RECOVERING LOST GROUND

*A Christian 12 Step Guide To Wholeness
And Wellbeing*

by

David P. Therrien

Copyright 2010 by David P. Therrien

In the U.S. write
David P. Therrien
1436 G.A.R. Highway
Swansea, MA 02777

Find me on Facebook at David Therrien, Rumford, RI

www.Inspiringbooks.org

Email
Inspiringbooksofhope@gmail.com

ISBN –1469937115

ISBN -13: 9781469937113

DEDICATION

Dedicated to those who admit their shortcomings and failures and pursue God to find forgiveness, healing and restoration. This book has been written with you in mind.

And to Matt Martin and Angie Snell who have dedicated themselves to helping people to recover lost ground.

RECOVERING LOST GROUND

How To Recover The Ground You've Lost Through Compulsive Behaviors

A Christian 12 Step Guide To Wholeness And Wellbeing

Use this book for your own private reading or read it together in a small group or book club.
There is a DVD and CD set of teachings available that accompany this book.
Go to www.inspiringbooks.org

David P. Therrien

CONTENTS

ABOUT THIS BOOK

RECOVERING LOST GROUND

Overcoming Compulsive Behaviors

Recovering lost ground is that act by which we gain back what we have lost due to compulsive behaviors. Compulsive behaviors are those destructive behaviors that control us. They dictate to us and rob us of our freedom to choose for ourselves. You don't have to be in this world very long before things begin to try to control you, rather than you control things. They are classified as "addictions." We want to be a people whose thoughts govern our lives, not be governed by our reactions.

Though there are many kinds of addictions that people struggle with, some are legal and some are illegal, there are also addictions that go unheeded such as judging, gossiping, and other relational evils.

This series of teachings is intended to help you to identify your compulsive behaviors, if you haven't already, and to find the strength and freedom from them that God provides. So if you are ready, let's begin to recover that lost ground that you have lost through compulsive behaviors.

Introduction
Believe That God
Can Do This

INTRODUCTION

Believe That God Can Do This

In order for any changes to come into our lives, we have to have a belief system that says God is able to bring those changes. We have to believe that God can do things in our lives that we cannot do ourselves. And we have to live as if only God can do these things.

So I ask myself, as I look at my struggles "Do I believe that God can do this?" What is the struggle in my life? What is the battle I am constantly fighting?

My struggle is:

____

____

Here is the way it works.
1. Look at your resources.
2. Do what God says with it.
3. Stand back and watch the miracle.
These simple steps can be life-changing.

John 2 will afford us the opportunity to see how this works.
This is the first recorded miracle of Jesus in the Gospels.

Background to the story:
There is a wedding reception going on. The bride and groom have made their vows and committed themselves to one another.
The food is being served and the wine is flowing. Everyone is having a good time. Jesus and His disciples were also invited to the wedding.
Then it happened.
v. 3 *When the wine ran out...*
This was an awful thing to have happen.
Let's try to understand a Middle Eastern Wedding. It was a very notable occasion. The wedding would be an open house in the home of the bride and groom. People would come and go all week long, celebrating the wedding.

The Ancients taught, "Where there was no wine, there was no joy," though they despised drunkenness. They believed a person should always be in control. Being in control is a virtue. Their wine was mixed with water to dilute it. Hospitality was a sacred duty; therefore, it would be humiliating to run out of wine.

v.3 The mother of Jesus said to Him, "They have no wine."

v.4 And Jesus said to her, "Ma'am, what does that have to do with us? My hour has not yet come."

v.5 His mother said to the servants, "Whatever He says to you, do it."

It appears that Mary had something to do with the arrangements. Older manuscripts say Mary was a relative, perhaps an aunt to the groom, she being the sister of the groom's mother. She also had the authority to order the servants. Note v.5.

Now, Jesus goes to work:

v.6 Now there were six stone water pots set there for the Jewish custom of purification, containing twenty or thirty gallons each.

v.7 Jesus said to them, "Fill the water pots with water." So they filled them up to the brim.

v.8 And He said to them, "Draw some out now and take it to the headwaiter." So they took it to him.

v.9 When the headwaiter tasted the water which had become wine, and did not know where it came from (but the servants who had drawn the water knew), the headwaiter called the bridegroom.

Isn't it interesting that the servants knew where the new wine came from but the headwaiter did not? This shows us that people who are close to Christ have a greater understanding of what God is doing than those who are not so close to Him.

So, if you really want to know the workings of God, stay close to Him. The servants knew what Jesus was doing because they were a part of it.

The best thing to do in this life is to participate in the work of God. There are so many things in this life that we can be involved with but the best thing to be involved with is the work of God on planet earth.

The headwaiter, after tasting the water which had become wine said;

v.10 *"Every man serves the good wine first, and when the people have drunk freely, then he serves the poorer wine; but you have kept the good wine until now."*

Jesus could have worked His first miracle anywhere, doing anything. Isn't it interesting that He used a wedding and He turned water into wine for His first miracle.

What can we learn from this first miracle?

1. Jesus wants people to have joy; not disappointment.

There is a difference between joy and happiness. Happiness is based on circumstances. Joy is based on knowing God, trusting God and walking with God. Happiness is more outwardly dependent, where joy is more inwardly focused. We find happiness on the outside, but we find joy on the inside.

2. The miracle happened where there was a need. Jesus chose to do His first miracle where the need was legitimate.

3. It saved a family from humiliation.

God doesn't want His people to be humiliated or embarrassed. When someone enters into a compulsive, destructive behavior, it embarrasses the whole family. No one sins to themselves. Whoever sins, affects those in the home or those who are in a close relationship. Jesus doesn't want to just restore an individual but He wants the whole family to be restored.

Application:

What can we learn from this first miracle to better our lives?

1. Look at your resources

This wedding was a place where there was a legitimate need. We can come to a place in life where the need can be great.

Remember, we are talking about overcoming compulsive behaviors. And where did these compulsive behaviors come from? They began with a series of choices. In the beginning the choices were yours. But as time went on, you started losing your ability to choose. Your behavior started choosing for you. That's what makes it a compulsive behavior.

In the story, what resources did we have? We had six stone water pots. Six is the number for imperfection and for man, for man was created on the sixth day. This is a picture of man's heart before Jesus fills it. It is empty and void of true joy. The empty, stony, water pot is a picture of people, born into this world empty of God. It is God's desire that He would fill each and every one of us with Himself.

You might be broken or empty, even feeling like you've been cast aside. Yet, if this is the best you have to offer to God, He will take it.

You see, God is not looking for people to offer to Him a person that is completely put together. No, God is looking for people to offer themselves to Him that need to be put together. God does His best work with broken people, empty people. That is why, when you become a victim of a compulsive behavior, God can do His best work in your life. It's better to be empty than full. When we are full of our own stuff, nothing of God can get in.

But when we come to God and we are empty, then we have a capacity to be filled by God.

2. Do what God says

v.7 *Jesus said to them, "Fill the water pots with water." So they filled them up to the brim.*

Notice how it is specified that they "filled the pots to the brim." "Filled to the brim" means to give God your full capacity. When you give yourself to God, don't hold anything back. As much as you give to God, that is how much He can work with on your behalf.

Here is someone that needs help from God. They cry out, "God, help me. Deliver me. I am a slave to this behavior. I don't know what to do. The more I try to come out from under it, the more it controls me."

So what do you do? You give to God all of yourself. Don't hold anything back. The more you give to God of yourself, the more He can work with on your behalf. That's because you're giving Him more to work with.

Jesus was given six water pots to work with. Each water pot was filled with twenty to thirty gallons of water. Let's make it twenty-five gallons. That equals one hundred and fifty gallons of water turned into one hundred and fifty gallons of wine. I am not aware of a wedding that would exhaust that supply of wine.

This is a picture of what the Apostle Paul said in II Corinthians 12:9; "His grace is sufficient..." In other words, there is always more than enough.

We have to remember that there is more than enough of God for Him to give Himself to every person and there will still be plenty left over. But God is not stingy when He gives Himself to a person. And He is asking that we would not be stingy when we give ourselves to Him.

v.8 *Jesus said to them, "<u>Draw some out</u> now and take it to the headwaiter." So they took it to him.*

This was an act of faith; to draw water out of a water pot and expect it to become wine.

Do you remember the question that was asked in the beginning? "Do you believe that God can do this?"

The servants had to have faith because they took large pots filled with water and brought them to the headwaiter without seeing the change. At what point did the water become wine? We don't know but what really matters is their faith to do what Jesus told them to do. It was an act of faith to believe that Jesus was going to take just plain, common water and turn it, not only into wine but the best wine they ever tasted.

There are many wonderful things that happen in the lives of people that believe in God's Word, even though natural thinking doubts. It's amazing the testimonies that many people have concerning how Jesus changed their lives. And they only had to do one thing. They believed in the Word of God.

Here is the principle:

When you believe in the Word of God, you act on what the Word of God says. Believing the Word of God is not just Bible study. It is certainly not winning a theological argument. Believing the Word of God is coming under the authority of the Word, doing what it says, believing it and obeying it by faith, and then trusting that God will bring out a positive outcome. The Bible is filled with stories of people who took God at His Word and He came through for them in a beautiful way.

Sometimes natural thinking doubts. But faith says I am going to overcome my natural thinking. Faith is contrary to natural thinking.

By faith, the Israelites crossed the Red Sea. By faith, Joshua took the city of Jericho by believing that God, Himself would bring down the walls. Extraordinary belief in what God says will cause extraordinary things to happen.

If I am going to be a person that lives in faith, I must overcome my doubts. It must become a lifestyle. Faith is like a muscle and therefore it takes a lifestyle of believing for faith to develop, just like your physical muscle. No one goes to the gym once a month and expects their muscles to grow. It must become a part of their way of life. And so it is with believing God. It must be a way of life, a lifestyle. Then, it is at that point that you can say, "I believe that God can do this."

Then.

3. Stand back and watch the miracle

v.10   *The headwaiter said to him, "Every man serves the good wine first, and when the people have drunk freely, then he serves the poorer wine; but you have kept the good wine until now."*

This story does not advocate drinking. It is a metaphor, taken from ancient Jewish culture in which Jesus lived, to demonstrate how God can bring deliverance and joy to a stony, empty vessel. In your own life. God wants you to know that, in spite of what you have gone through in the past, He saves the best for last.

Jesus is not teaching us how to throw a dinner party or a wedding by saving the good wine until the end. He is teaching us that in our own lives, we will do all kinds of things our way. You can go here and go there. Buy this and buy that. You can eat that, drink that, and inject that. You can marry this one and sleep with that one. You can "go for all of the gusto" if you choose. You are a free will agent. You can live your life any way you choose to.

Then, He often waits until our resources are completely exhausted or run out, like those empty stone water pots. Those water pots had better days. They were now completely empty. You would look at them and say, those things are useless. They're not holding any water. The only good water pot is a water pot with water in it. It's like an ice cube tray that no one put any water into it. When you went for some ice, the tray was empty. (If you remember those days).

So what good are empty ice cube trays when you need ice? They are no good. And what good are empty water pots when you need water? They are no good. They both look completely useless.

Now, if you are like that when you come to God, God will take you. In your mind, you have bottomed out. You've burned your bridges. People have given up on you. You've got no where to turn. That compulsive behavior has gotten the best of you. And people are tired of you. They are tired of your excuses, your alibis and lies. Some have even said, "Don't call me."

But God says, "I will take you like you are." God is saying, "If I can take an empty, stone water pot and fill that thing with joy, I can take your life, as broken and bruised as it is, and I can do the very same thing."

So God lets us live our lives right into the pit because sometimes it is only in the pit that we look up and we find God. (*See my book, "Look Up And Be Forgiven. at inspiringbooks.org*) Then we can actually give ourselves to God. He can begin to do the work of reshaping, rebuilding and putting us back together again.

We would do better for ourselves if we sought help before the crisis. We would do better if we sought help before that thing became an addiction, or before the divorce or the bankruptcy. You can fill in the blank with whatever you like.

It is always better to get help when you see the problem arising but sometimes we are blind to it. You wake up one day and realize, I am a slave to alcohol. I am a slave to gambling. I am a slave to lust or drugs. The list goes on. I am a slave to shopping! You would be amazed at how many people find comfort in shopping and eating. But when Jesus is asked for help, He does more than we could ever ask or think.

What was it that got Jesus moving to remedy the situation at the wedding? The answer is simple. He was asked. His mother came to Him and told Him someone needed His help. He stepped right in and He helped. All you need to do is ask God. He is ready and willing to help you. Jesus hears the one who acknowledges their problem; the one who knows they have a need.

Key verse:

v.5 *His mother said to the servants, "Whatever He says to you, do it."* I don't care what He says, whatever He says, do it. But if you don't do what He says, the right outcome will not be realized.

That works with us the very same way. You can bring your need to God, but if you don't do what He says, you're never going to get the outcome you are looking for. You will not receive the victory. Then, you will remain in your state of humiliation.

That's why faith says God is going to tell me to do some things that might not make sense to my natural thinking, but I'm going to trust Him. I'm going to believe that throughout the whole Bible, God told people to do things that seemed strange, but they obeyed and they had an amazing outcome every time.

I ask myself, "Why would I be any different? I'm going to trust God for what He says to me. And I'm going to trust Him for the same amazing outcome."

Now, what was the most important reason Jesus did this miracle?

v.11 *This beginning of His signs Jesus did in Cana of Galilee, and manifested His glory, and His disciples <u>believed in Him</u>.*

We know that the disciples had a degree of faith in Jesus. After all, they left their fishing boats to follow Him. Just like many people today have a degree of faith in Jesus. Many people go to church on Christmas Eve or Day, even if that is the only time of year they go. They have a degree of faith. But Jesus wants a little bit of faith to turn into confirmed faith. Confirmed faith is a faith that doesn't have any doubt mixed in with it. A lot of our faith has a little doubt mixed in with it. We say things like, "Yes, I know what I should do God, but..."

Jesus wanted the faith of the disciples to be confirmed because He was going to take them on a journey. Oh, this journey was much more challenging than a wedding. This journey was going to put their faith to the test so He used a wedding to get them to believe that they are following the right One.

We asked at the beginning, Do you believe that God can do this?

Do you believe that God can do this for you? At one time you had control, but through a series of poor choices, you became addicted. You turned into an empty, old, stone water pot. Do you believe that God can take an empty, hard and useless life and turn it into a means of great joy? You have to believe that, if you are going to let Him do it. He did it at a wedding. He can do it for anyone.

God is looking for opportunities to do something in the lives of people. This world is filled with Humpty Dumpty's. Oh, they're having a great time up on the wall. How long was Humpty Dumpty up there on that wall? We don't know. He could have been up there for years. Then he got a little too comfortable. He started rocking and rolling a little too much. And before you knew it, Humpty Dumpty had a great fall.

Well, the world had its resources didn't it? Yet, "All the king's horses and all the king's men couldn't put Humpty Dumpty back together again." But Jesus Christ can! And if you think you line up with Humpty Dumpty, it's okay. It's not the end of the world for you.

All you need to do is:

1. Look at your resources. What do you have that God can work with? You've got a broken, empty hard vessel that everybody already thinks is totally useless and good for nothing. Well, you bring that to God. Then...

2. Do what God says. Follow His Word. Accept the challenge. Trust that God knows what He is talking about. He created you and wired you. He knows what

makes you tick. He knows how to heal you and put you back together again.

Finally, stand back and watch the miracle. Watch your empty vessel begin to fill up with the wine of God and the joy of life. All through the Bible wine speaks of joy. God wants your life to be filled with joy. And only He can do it. But you have to do your part. You have to present yourself to Him. It doesn't matter what condition you are in. Just do it.

Abide in what He says to do. He will give the best recommendation for going forward, even if your natural thinking disagrees. Step back and watch God begin to heal and put you back together again. The joy, the purpose and significance will begin to come back into your life. Only God can do that but it takes believing that He can do it in order for that to happen.

Things I need to do

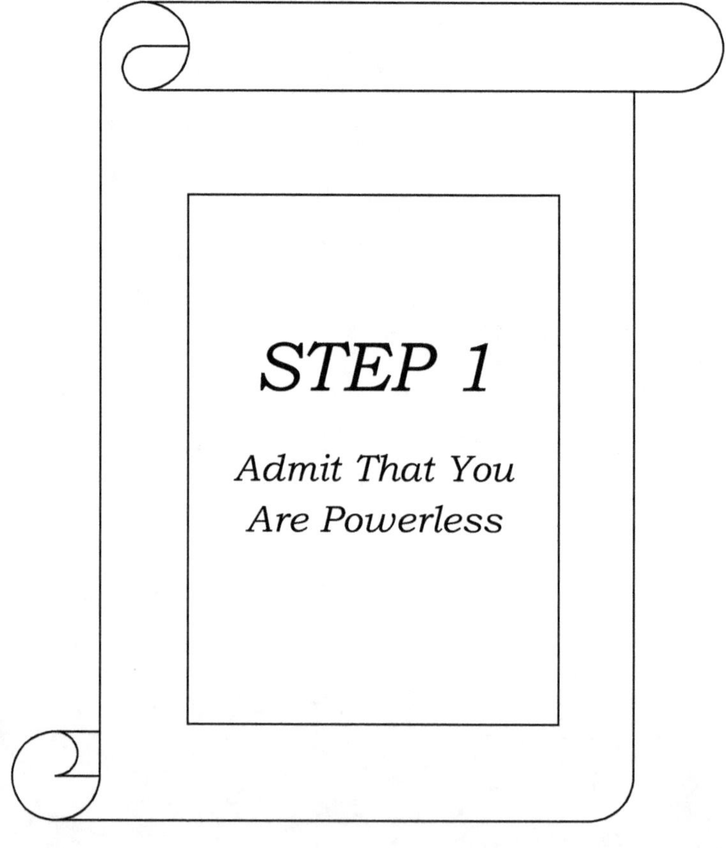

STEP 1

Admit That You
Are Powerless

STEP 1
Admit That You Are Powerless
A No Win Situation

In the introduction we learned that, in order for real change to take place in your life, you have to believe that God can do it.

We saw that Jesus took some empty water pots, filled them with water, and then turned them into the wine of joy. You have to believe that He can do that with you. He can take your emptiness, fill it and turn it into joy.

Have you ever been in what is called "a no win situation?" It is a place in life where, as it says, you just can't win. No matter what you do or say, you are powerless to bring the victory. It could be your station in life at home, or at work, maybe on the team. This place makes you feel trapped by the demands of others. Sometimes the phrase, "This isn't fair!" wells up in your mind. Maybe at work you think, "Why should I have to do that? I don't get paid for that. That's not my job description." But, if you want to keep your job, you have to do it. It's a no win situation. Or at home you may say, "That's not my responsibility. I already worked all day. Where I come from, husbands do this and wives do that." Even on the team you ask, "Why am I on the bench? I'm so much better than that other guy." Why am I on the bench?"

In these situations, you may feel completely powerless. You don't have anything in you by which you can change it. It is a no win situation. But when you believe that God can change it, He will.

THE STORY

Hagar is a picture of powerlessness. She was a servant to Abram and Sarah, so her rights were nonexistent.

Genesis 15:1-5 ...The word of the LORD came to Abram in a vision, saying, *"Do not fear. Abram said, "O Lord GOD, what will You give me, since I am childless, and the heir of my house is Eliezer of Damascus?"*

Remember, God told Abram he would be the father of a great nation. Yet, at this time, he is ninety years old and has no children.

And Abram said, "Since You have given no offspring to me, one born in my house is my heir."

Then behold, the word of the LORD came to him, saying, "This man will not be your heir; but one who will come forth from your own body, he shall be your heir."

Notice how this theme keeps returning. You have to believe that God can do it. Abram is on in years, past the point of having children. Sarah is only ten years younger and certainly past the age of childbearing. So, in order for this to happen, they've got to believe that God can do it. They've got to believe that God can take empty vessels, fill them with His life and turn them into joy.

Then, God gave Abram a lesson from nature. Nature is a wonderful teacher of the attributes of God. Let's assume it was a beautiful, cloudless night.

And He took him outside and said, "Now look toward the heavens, and count the stars, if you are able to count them." And He said to him, "So shall your descendants be."

God uses a lesson from nature to get Abram to understand the significance of the promise. There are many lessons foe us in nature as well.

SQUIRREL STORY

I have a small, above ground pool in my backyard. One Sunday morning, as my wife was getting ready for church, she looked through the window and noticed a squirrel, drowning in the pool. He was going down for the count, on his last breath. She ran outside, got the net, lifted him out of the pool and laid him on the ground. He was almost lifeless. When she got home that day after church, the squirrel was gone. She told me the story and we celebrated that the little guy learned his lesson, God had given him grace and a second chance at life.

The next day she came home and saw a dead squirrel in the pool! Was it the same one? I don't know, but it probably was. The point is, sometimes we just don't learn. Sometimes we do things and God delivers us but we don't learn and go right back to that thing again. Sometimes this pattern is repeated over and over.

The danger is that there may come a time when God will not deliver anymore, like He did with the squirrel. So look at nature and see it as the wonderful teaching tool that it is and learn how God works and the grace that He gives us.

We now come to Genesis 16 and God is certainly taking His time fulfilling the promise of the child. Sarah, Abram's wife took matters into her own hands. Ten years later, still childless, she took Hagar, her servant girl and gave her to her husband to have the promised child. Their thought was, "Okay, if God is not going to make it happen, then we'll make it happen."

You never want to get in the way of God. You never want to doubt what He says He is going to do.

Well, Hagar had the child but Sarah became very jealous and made life impossible for Hagar. She treated her very cruelly. Unfortunately, Hagar did bring some of this upon herself. Let's read the account.

Genesis 16:4 *He went in to Hagar, and she conceived; and when she saw that she had conceived, her mistress was despised in her sight.*

This means that Hagar now despised Sarah, her mistress. You could say Hagar was "strutting her stuff." Sarah then blamed her husband for the mess.

v.5 *And Sarah said to Abram, "May the wrong done me be upon you. I gave my maid into your arms, but when she saw that she had conceived, I was despised in her sight. May the LORD judge between you and me."*

We often blame others when we are not happy with our circumstances.

Did you ever think to yourself, "I am not happy with my circumstances. Who can I blame for my unhappiness? Because I'm not happy, it must be somebody's fault. It can't be mine." That is exactly what Sarah did. Sarah thought to herself, "I don't like what's going on here. Let me go blame my husband." She forgot it was her idea in the first place to give her maid to her husband.

v.6 *But Abram said to Sarah, "Behold, your maid is in your power; do to her what is good in your sight." So Sarah treated her harshly, and Hagar fled from her presence.*

Yes, Hagar was a type of victim, but she added to her dilemma by being proud and arrogant. This is the beginning of the slippery slope of compulsive behaviors.

What is it that brings a person to a place where they do things, and they know it's probably not the right thing to do, but it's the thing that they do anyway? Sometimes the thing that they do becomes more controlling than their own thoughts. It just may be from living in an attitude of pride and arrogance. That is the beginning.

Pride comes before the fall. (Proverbs 11:2)

You think, how did that person get way down there? Someone answers, well, when they were over here, they were very prideful and arrogant. You couldn't tell them anything. And pride comes before the fall. It's a slippery slope, and there they are. The Book of James tells us, *God resists the proud, but He exalts the humble."* (James 4:6)

How did Hagar handle her problem? <u>She ran away</u>.

Today, people also find themselves in a place where they feel victimized, they are in a no win situation, like Hagar, and they run. And where do they run to? Some run to:

- Alcohol – this will help me to deal with it
- Drugs – this will help me feel better
- Gambling – this will make me rich and solve my problems
- Shopping – this will give me joy
- Denial – this is not really happening
- Eating – this is real comforting
- Judging others – I'm not as bad as them.
- ____________________________

fill in your own

Eventually, these things control your thinking. All of these things get our mind off the real problem – ourselves. The object or goal of the Christian life is to become like Christ. But here is the difficult part. On the way to Christlikeness, there is a lot of soul searching that we have to do. Introspection is part of the journey.

Unfortunately, many people are in the sport of looking at others, rather than looking at themselves. It is only by looking at yourself that you can make the necessary changes to become more Christlike.

Hagar is in a no win situation. She is despised by her family; Abram and Sarah being her only family, and now she is homeless. She has no support system and she is feeling sorry for herself. There is nothing she can do on her own to make things better.

THE BREAKTHROUGH

Sometimes, this is the best place to be.

When we are powerless, God is powerful. But as long as we are full of our own stuff, God can't move in and fill us. That is why when Jesus turned water into wine He said, "Get six empty pots." Pride and arrogance prevents my being filled by God because I am already full of my own stuff.

Many people who arrive in this place, stay there. They actually accept the status in life where they say, "I'll stay here. I'll stay an alcoholic. I'll remain a gambler, shopaholic, over-eater" or what have you. They say, "I'll stay at this place in life because I don't have what it takes to break out of this behavior, so this is where I'll spend the rest of my life."

But the breakthrough is to realize that God loves everybody! God loves us even when we don't love Him. God loves us and He never stops loving us. He does everything He can do to draw us back to Him. But sometimes in our pride, we don't see it. That's why Hagar was brought to a place where she had absolutely nothing going for her. This is where she heard the voice of God.

v.7-9 *Now the angel of the LORD* (Jesus) *found her by a spring of water in the wilderness, by the spring on the way to Shur.*

He said, "Hagar, Sarah's maid, where have you come from and where are you going?" And she said, "I am fleeing from the presence of my mistress Sarah."

Hagar said, "I'm running. I'm running away." This is what people do. They don't like their circumstances so they run away. I don't like the way my marriage is going so I'm going to - run away. I don't like the way my work is going so I'm going to – run away. Whatever it is that we don't like is happening, we become very good at running away from it. But when you run from your problems, you are taking the problem with you!

v.9 Then the angel of the LORD said to her, *"Return to your mistress, and submit yourself to her authority."*

God gave her two things to do:

1. Return to where she ran from.

2. Submit to her masters.

Now, God knows everything. He knew everything that happened to Hagar. One Bible translation even says that Sarah beat Hagar. Now, did God see that? Yes He did. And what did He say?

He said to go back to the place that you ran from. Fleeing from it doesn't solve it. So let's rewind and go back to where it all began. God continued, <u>When you get back there, submit to her authority.</u>

The natural minded person would really struggle with this command. We must remember God's ways are not natural, but supernatural. This is how to avoid the slippery slope of compulsive behaviors.

We have to do the hard work. It's cheaper to build a house than to renovate a house. When you build a house, you start from scratch with a clean lot. When you renovate a house, you have to first undo a lot of stuff before you can build the new stuff. You have to remove a lot of the old house before you can rebuild the new house. And the conditions are not that easy because you have to work around the old stuff.

God is in the process of rebuilding you. He gave you a life and you almost destroyed it with poor choices.

So God wants to make you new and this remodeling is a lot of work.

God told Hagar to return to where she ran from because running doesn't solve anything. She is to humble herself and resume her previous role as a servant.

You also have to believe that God can do what He says He is going to do by doing what He says. If God says to go get six empty water pots, then go get six empty water pots. Don't mumble. Don't complain. Don't say, "What do I have to get six empty water pots for?" Just do it and let God work the miracle.

Now I have to ask myself, "Do I have that kind of faith?" Do I have the kind of faith that when God tells me to do something I go right out and do it? Or do I say, "That's the last thing I want to do." Or do I have the kind of faith where I'm going to trust God, do what He says, then step back and watch the miracle? This is the **first step** on my road to recovery.

v.10 *Moreover, the angel of the LORD said to her, "I will greatly multiply your descendants so that they will be too many to count."*

God is saying, Hagar, do you remember that promise that I gave to Abram? Well, I'm giving you the same promise. I am going to give you descendants that you cannot number. And Ishmael, her son from Abram, actually did become the leader of a great nation and that nation has been the enemy of Israel ever since.

v.13 *Hagar thought, "Have I really seen God and lived to tell about it?" So from then on she called him, "The God Who Sees Me."* (Contemporary English Version)

Hagar attached this name to God because people believed that if anyone saw God they would be consumed by God's righteousness. She called Him, "The God Who Looks After Me." (The English Standard Version)

I was a victim. I was treated unfairly. I was abused. I chose to flee away. God was looking after me every step of the way. God followed me, He sought me out, and He found me. He instructed me, and then God blessed me. He also gave me a promise.

Do you see how it all works? God never gives up on us. He has instructions for us. And if we are really serious about the victory, we have to follow by faith the instructions that God gives. God knows exactly what it takes to get it done. We don't know what it takes, that's why we try all kinds of things but to no avail.

THE LESSON:

You may find yourself in a no win situation where things are beyond your control. You may be tempted to run away by means of alcohol, drugs, gambling, shopping, blaming others or any other way to ease the pain.

What you escape to today may be the thing you escape from tomorrow.

Sometimes we hurt so much that we do something to ease the pain. But the thing that we do often causes even more pain. And yet, we give our life to that thing. It becomes our new companion. We let it have control over us where we used to have control.

If you want your life back, this is where it begins. Realize that God will meet you in your pain and when He does, He has a promise for you.

God didn't find Hagar and rebuke her saying, "You get back there you little slave girl. Where do you think you're going?" No, not at all. He met her in her pain. It was like He felt what she felt. That's because when you love someone so much, when they hurt, you hurt. So when we hurt, God hurts. If you stop running and let God meet you, He has a special promise for you. For Hagar, it was that her son would be the leader of a great nation. For you, well, you have to sit and listen to God.

Things I need to do

39

STEP 2

*Believe A Power
Greater Than
Yourself Can
Restore You*

STEP 2
Believe A Power Greater Than Yourself
Can Restore You
Arrogant Thinking

When under the control of one's addiction, it is common to deny the truth about the situation. Arrogant thinking or prideful thinking is blinding. This thinking blinds us to truth and separates us from people.

We will learn in this lesson;

Pr 29:23 *A man's pride will bring him low, But a humble spirit will obtain honor.*

Daniel 4 Background

Nebuchadnezzar was the king of ancient Babylon. He was the most powerful ruler on earth at that time. He also thought himself to be a god. Yet, with all of this, he lacked the most important thing, peace. Nebuchadnezzar will show us when a man is unhappy with himself he becomes hostile toward the people around him.

We will look at two phases of Nebuchadnezzar's life.

Phase I.

The king had a great statue of himself constructed and demanded the worship of the people. (Now that's insecurity)

There were three Hebrew boys who refused to bow down in worship. They were thrown into a fiery furnace but the Lord met them there. They came out unscathed, without even the trace of smoke upon them.

Note the king's response;

Daniel 3:28 *Nebuchadnezzar responded and said, "Blessed be the God of Shadrach, Meshach and Abed-nego, who has sent His angel and delivered His servants who put their trust in Him, violating the king's command, and yielded up their bodies so as not to serve or worship any god except their own God.*

v.29 Therefore I make a decree that any people, nation or tongue that speaks anything offensive against the God of Shadrach, Meshach and Abed-nego shall be torn limb from limb and their houses reduced to a rubbish heap, inasmuch as there is no other god who is able to deliver in this way."

The king even gave them a promotion at work! He gave them high offices in his court.

Now, this may look like a breakthrough but we will see it is really not.

Nebuchadnezzar is in a place that many people are today, perhaps even some of you. Notice what the king said.

"Blessed be the God of Shadrach, Meshach and Abed-nego,

There is no other god who is able to deliver in this way."

Sounds good doesn't it? After all, he is acknowledging the existence of God. Watch!

In Daniel 4 Nebuchadnezzar had a dream. He dreamed a tree grew up so high that the whole world could see it. It's leaves were fresh and green and the tree was filled with fruit so much so, that the world was fed from it. Wild animals rested in its shade and birds sheltered in its branches. But an angel soon came down and gave the order to cut down the tree, scatter its fruit, and scatter the animals and birds from it. But he said to leave the stump. Band it with a chain of iron and brass.

Then it got really personal for the king.

Daniel 4:15 *Yet leave the stump with its roots in the ground, but with a band of iron and bronze around it. In the new grass of the field; let him be drenched with the dew of heaven, and let him share with the beasts in the grass of the earth.*

v.16 *Let his mind be changed from that of a man And let a beast's mind be given to him, And let seven periods of time pass over him.*

v.17 *This sentence is by the decree of the {angelic} <u>watchers</u> and the decision is a command of the holy ones, in order that the living may know that the Most High is ruler over the realm of mankind, and bestows it on whom He wishes and sets over it the lowliest of men."*

The "Watchers" are angels who watch over the affairs of mankind.

So, Nebuchadnezzar brought this dream to his magicians, astrologers, fortune-tellers and wizards but none of them could interpret the dream. Then, he brought it to Daniel, who is also called Belteshazzar.

v.18 *This is the dream which I, King Nebuchadnezzar, have seen. Now you, Belteshazzar, tell me its interpretation, inasmuch as none of the wise men of my kingdom is able to make known to me the interpretation; but you are able, for a spirit of the holy gods is in you.'*

Daniel was silent for about an hour, for he was stunned at the dream. Then he said to the king, you are the tree.

v.25 The interpretation

You will be driven away from mankind and your dwelling place will be with the beasts of the field, and you will be given grass to eat like cattle and be drenched with the dew of heaven; and seven periods of time (years) will pass over you, until you recognize that the Most High is ruler over the realm of mankind and bestows it on whomever He wishes.

He told him the stump would be left to give the king another chance, should he repent of his arrogance.

Now, Nebuchadnezzar had a whole year to think about his pride problem.

v.29 *Twelve months later he was walking on the roof of the royal palace of Babylon.*

v.30 *The king reflected and said, "Is this not Babylon the great, which I myself have built as a royal residence by the might of my power and for the glory of my majesty?"*

Now, what is up with Nebuchadnezzar? He just got a warning from God, but to no avail.

Sound familiar? Is this part of the way we think too?

v.33 *Immediately the word concerning Nebuchadnezzar was fulfilled; and he was driven away from mankind and began eating grass like cattle, and his body was drenched with the dew of heaven until his hair had grown like eagles' feathers and his nails like birds' claws.*

Remember our proverb? *A man's pride will bring him low, But a humble spirit will obtain honor.* Pr 29:23

For Nebuchadnezzar, it did; and it will.

Now, the breakthrough.

Here is where Step 2 can become a reality:

"Believe A Power Greater Than Yourself

Can Restore You"

Phase II:

V.34 *But at the end of that period, I, Nebuchadnezzar, raised my eyes toward heaven and my reason returned to me,*

When he looked to heaven, his sanity returned.

and I blessed the Most High and praised and honored Him who lives forever; For His dominion is an everlasting dominion, And His kingdom endures from generation to generation.

He realizes the power of God:

V.35 *All the inhabitants of the earth are accounted as nothing, but He does according to His will in the host of heaven And among the inhabitants of earth; and no one can ward off His hand or say to Him, 'What have You done?'*

His humility was rewarded:

v.36 *At that time my reason returned to me. And my majesty and splendor were restored to me for the glory of my kingdom, and my counselors and my nobles began seeking me out; so I was reestablished in my sovereignty, and surpassing greatness was added to me.*

Here comes the big one, this didn't happen previously.

v.37 *"Now I, Nebuchadnezzar, praise, exalt and honor the King of heaven, for all His works are true and His ways just, and He is able to humble those who walk in pride."*

Remember Daniel ch.3?

Daniel 3:28 Nebuchadnezzar said, "Blessed be the God of Shadrach, Meshach and Abednego who has delivered his servants. He then made a decree for all his subjects to worship the God of the Hebrew boys.

But the king didn't make it personal for himself. Now, in Ch. 4 He says; *"Now I, Nebuchadnezzar, praise, exalt and honor the King of heaven,* v.37. God has now become personal with him.

You see, there is a danger in just acknowledging the power and sovereignty of God, without a personal relationship with Him.

Nebuchadnezzar was strong in that he accomplished much as a great king. He was weak in that he was insecure and became a demanding individual. His pride blinded him to the truth about himself.

What he teaches us:

1. God's power goes to those who submit to His will.

2. Refusal to God's perfect will creates animal instincts within us.

3. True peace only comes from putting our lives in God's hands.

4. Healing comes when we admit our sin and realize that His power can restore us.

Things I need to do

STEP 3

*We Made A
Decision To Turn
Our Will And Life
Over To The Care
Of God*

STEP 3
Turn Your Will and Life Over to God
Freedom to Choose

What is the danger of a compulsive behavior? Some people have compulsive behaviors which literally threaten their lives. They put their life on a road to devastation. Compulsive behaviors come in all levels but we know one thing. Jesus died to set the captive free. We were all born into the world, captive by sin. Through faith in Christ and salvation in the new birth we can become free, but there is still a learning curve that enables us to experience the freedom that God provides. Hopefully, this book will bring to you the way to attain that freedom.

We noted in step one, the first step of the journey is to admit that you are powerless to change things. We are not all that we think we are and when we start to think too highly of ourselves, God has a way of bringing us back to reality doesn't He? Not only does He bring you back to reality, which He is very good at, but in that process, He humbles us and that's okay because when He humbles us, we will no longer see the greatness of ourselves. It is through humility that we see the greatness of God.

So Step 1 is a reminder that I don't have the power to get out of this mess.

In Step 2 we remember that we came to believe that there is a power greater than ourselves and this power restores us to sanity. Of course we identify the power to be Jesus Christ, not some higher power that has no name. We know Who the power is.

We looked at the life of Nebuchadnezzar and we saw the phases of the good king's life. The king started off in a place of what we call arrogant thinking. He thought so highly of himself and maybe because of a degree of insecurity at the same time, he had a giant statue built of himself. Now, you have to be overly proud and overly insecure when you have a giant statue built of yourself as an object of worship. To make matters worse, the king put this orchestra together and he said to everyone in his kingdom, "When you hear the sound of the music bow down and worship my statue." It is going to be seen that God had some big plans for Nebuchadnezzar. This is a good thing because if God has big plans for somebody He is not going to leave them to their own devices. Think about that. If God has big plans for you, He is not going to leave you to your own devices. He is going to intervene in your life. He is going to take you to school. He might even take you to the woodshed. But He will intervene like He did with Nebuchadnezzar.

Nebuchadnezzar began with arrogant thinking but he was ultimately humbled by God. And if you remember the account, he was given the mind of an animal. Arrogance will do that. Arrogance will affect the way that you think and turn you into an animal. He found himself out in the field eating grass like an ox. This went on for seven years. The Bible says that after seven years, for some reason, he looked up to heaven and he acknowledged God. As a result, God restored his thinking to sane thinking. These are some of the phases that people can go through.

Step 3

We made a decision to turn our will and life over to the care of God as we understand it.

This simply means that we have options in our lives. God has given us the ability to choose options. Much of that choosing has to do with life and death. We don't often think how many of our choices have anything to do with life and death. But they actually do. We make choices everyday, answering the question, "Will I experience life or will I experience death?" Our choices affect the way we live. They can certainly bring a feeling of death into our circumstances. For instance, it has been said that a marriage can die because love dies. Now the question is, how did love die? How does love die between a man and a woman who make vows of commitment to one another? The answer is "choices." They chose how they would talk to each other. They chose how they would respond to each other. They chose whether they would or they would not understand each other and support each other. Choices mean everything.

A career can be alive or a career can be dead. It is all determined by the choices that we make. I can choose to put all of my heart into it or I can drag my feet.

This series is about compulsive behaviors, and in the midst of the compulsive behavior you have choices. You can choose to come out of that behavior or you can choose to remain in it. Coming out of it is not an overnight thing. It took a long time to get there and takes a long time to get out. But you can choose to start taking steps away from that compulsive behavior, whatever it might be.

God has given us freedom to choose which always brings results. Every choice has a result. Do you know what our lives are? Our lives are the sum total of the choices that we make. Our autobiography can be spelled out on a long piece of paper saying, these are the choices that I've made and how they shaped my life.

Where we are right now in our lives is because of the choices that we made yesterday. You might be right on top, you might be on the bottom, or somewhere in the middle. For the most part the choices that we made in the past have brought us to where we are in the present. That tells me that we have no one to blame but ourselves.

When I look at my life I know for a fact my life could be much more fulfilling, much more complete and much more rewarding. But it's not and that is because throughout my life I made bad choices. I think we can all basically agree to some level that we've all made some really good choices and some really bad choices. And choices determine where we are at our station in life.

Now in Deuteronomy chapter 30, God is well aware of this principle and for that reason He gave

Moses an important message for the people of Israel. [By the way, when we look at the people of Israel they were the people of God of that day. As we go through this book, remember that you are the people of God today. When God is talking to the people of God it means that we've got everything we need to carry out what He says. There is no excuse. We make excuses but there is absolutely no excuse in the world as to why we can't carry out the things that God says in His Word. There is no reason because we are the people of God. We've got the power, the promises and a protector. You've got God.]

Deuteronomy chapter 30:15 God is talking to the people of Israel through Moses. He said, *See I have set before you today life and prosperity and death and adversity.*

Now, that is interesting because you would think God sets before us life and the devil sets before us death. The devil just comes to steal, kill and destroy, but God comes to give life. God says, "I'm putting in front of you life and prosperity, death and adversity." I'm setting up a scenario where you can use the gift of your free will for your own benefit.

Now why did God even set up the scenario? Perhaps He wants us to see that man has a free will and it must be used. Don't waste your ability to think by living in how you feel. Half the time we go through life we are feeling our way through. Someone asks, Why did you do that?" Answer. "Because I felt like it." We let our feelings direct us. If you really want to get into trouble, let your feelings direct you. God says "No." "I want you to see the value of choice. And I want you to see that if you make good choices, your life will be blessed. And if you make bad choices, your life is going to be cursed." God has given us the gift of the free will and He wants us to use that gift to the best of our ability.

Now, another Bible translation, the Contemporary English Version says it like this. *Today I'm giving you a choice you can choose life and success or death and disaster.* And we answer when we choose life or death, or we choose success or disaster.

This type of thinking removes the "victim" mentality. God is saying, "My people will not go through life, saying, oh me oh my, why is this happening to me? Oh me oh my, why do I feel like this?" God is saying, "because you chose, that's why. You set yourself up. You feel like this because these are the feelings that you've accepted and you've entertained them. And you've given yourself over to them." If there is one thing you do not want to do it is to give your feelings control over you. Feelings are like a dog. You have to keep them on a leash.

How many of you have a dog with the leash that goes inside of the little holder with a pushbutton on the handle? When you walk the dog you let it out as far as you want. When he gets too far ahead, you push the button and the leash stops going out. Your feelings are like that. You let them out, bring them in. The best dog is a trained dog. Just like you want your dog under control, so it is with your feelings.

How many people are in jail because of their feelings? How many people are addicted because of how they felt? Compulsive behaviors grow in an environment with people who are controlled by their feelings. They are not thinking, they are feeling, and if they don't like the way they feel, they do something to change those feelings which is usually not good, even destructive. Then it becomes a bad, compulsive behavior.

People who struggle with compulsive behaviors make themselves victims and therefore it's always someone else's fault for their situation.

They say, "I'm like this because of him; because of her; because of them. It is never because of me."

Verse 16 God is speaking and He says;

v.16 *in that I command you today to love the LORD your God, to walk in His ways and to keep His commandments and His statutes and His judgments, that you may live and multiply, and that the LORD your God may bless you in the land where you are entering to possess it.*

God is saying I want you to choose life. Then He shows us what choosing life looks like.

Here is what choosing life looks like:

1. Love the Lord Your God
2. Walk in His ways – this is your course of life, plot it wisely. Study the Scriptures so you stay on course.
3. Keep His commandments – the laws of God. God gives me His laws for my own wellbeing. As the laws of the land protect us and our property, possessions and freedoms, the laws of God are given to protect us as well. We have a healthy society when we operate by those laws.
4. Keep His statutes – ordinances, customs
5. Keep His judgments – decrees

Simply put, it is a life yielded to God. To yield means to give the other one the right of way. Think of the yield sign on a ramp getting on to a highway. The driver with the yield sign is to let the other driver go first. We are called to live a life yielded to God. This is where the battle of the flesh begins.

Remember, we said; choices bring results.

that [for the purpose of] *you may live and multiply, and that the LORD your God may bless you in the land where you are entering to possess it.* v.16

How often do you stop to think of the blessings that God wants to bring your way? What do you think right now? Is God blessing you or are you in a place where He wants to bless you but your choices are preventing it?

A yielded life is a blessed life.

The people of God were going into the Land of Promise. Sometimes we call it the Promised Land. What did that look like? This land was their reward for faith and obedience. In that land, the vineyards were already planted. The houses were already built and the wells were already dug. They were moving into a place that was totally prepared for them, but by somebody else. It was called a land flowing with milk and honey, a picture of freedom and prosperity. They were the people of God, then. We are the people of God, today.

For us, it is a Land of Promises, a land that offers freedom and prosperity in a spiritual sense. The Land of Promises is the place where I live spiritually, and I am inundated with the promises of God. There are thousands of promises in His Word to encourage me, to motivate me and inspire me. They lift me up and put my feet upon a Rock (Jesus Christ). This is where God is leading us. He is leading us to a place where we feast on His promises. Think of it. The promises of God's Word are more real than the things that you experience in everyday life.

Every so often we have to ask ourselves, what promises am I living by? Am I living by any promises at all? When was the last time you grabbed one of God's promises and said this one is for me? This one will get me through the week. Or this promise will help me in this situation. We need to be educated in the promises of God. If you are not knowledgeable of the promises of God you are ill equipped for the battle. A quiver full of arrows is greater assurance of victory in the fight. An empty quiver is sure defeat. A Bible Promise book will fill your quiver. In it, He has promises for many circumstances of life. Then you can reach into your quiver and grab a promise for the immediate need. There are some Bible Promises reserved for you in the back of this book.

Ask yourself if you really believe that there is a promise reserved for you; that God has direction and hope reserved for you in His Word.

Our mantra for this chapter is:

Choices bring results. *(Read that again)*

We are not victims nor are we playing the blame game. Back in the Garden, Adam blamed Eve and Eve blamed the serpent. Everyone seems to blame someone else for what they did.

Here is another one:

My life is the sum total of the choices I've made. *(Read that again)*

The consequences:

v.17 *But if your <u>heart turns away</u> and you will <u>not</u> <u>obey</u>, but are <u>drawn away</u> and worship other gods and serve them,*

v.18 *I declare to you today that you shall surely perish.*

Let's go back to the little dog. When you take your dog for a walk, he loves to smell the neighborhood. I think the happiest dogs are those who ride in cars with the windows open. They are in their glory. Their keen sense of smell introduces them to a smorgasbord of fragrances.

Now, today we have leash laws because if you are not controlling your dog something else will draw him away, and when that happens, he will probably get into trouble. Either you are in control, or something else will be in control.

Just by "not" following what God says, something else will draw you away. God is saying that if your heart turns from Me, you will be drawn away by something else. We have been made to worship. Cultures all over the world worship. So what we worship is our choice.

v.17 *But if your <u>heart turns away</u>*

God begins with the heart because sin begins in the heart. Our decisions begin in the heart because our free will is in the heart. In your heart there is a compartment called the free will. The action is merely the outcome of the free will in the heart. The action is not the cause of the problem, the heart is the cause. The action is merely the result of the dictates of the heart.

To trace a behavior back to its origin, you've got to go to the heart. Solomon said, *As a man thinks in his heart, so is he.* (Proverbs 23:7) The real you is in the heart.

Here is the consequence of the wrong decision:

v.18 *You will not prolong your days in the land where you are crossing the Jordan to enter and possess it.*

God is saying, "I'm promising you long life, and if you don't take it, then you're going to have a short life.

Your life will be cut short even though you have all these promises before you." How sad is that?

So guard your heart. Protect your heart. Remember, garbage in - garbage out. What goes into your heart is what you use to think with.

Something happened. You didn't like it. It hurt you. You started thinking with your feelings. You didn't guard your heart. The result is a bad choice which becomes a series of bad choices and in the end, a compulsive behavior.

God reiterates:

v.19 *I call heaven and earth to witness against you today, that I have set before you life and death, the blessing and the curse.*

So choose life in order that you may live, you and your descendants,

But why is it that sometimes you don't choose life? Because you don't have life. You let circumstances dictate to you and tell you how to feel.

My boyfriend left me so my feelings are going to tell me that I must be lonely. My girlfriend left me so my feelings are telling me I am a reject, I have nothing to offer. Then I let those feelings lead me around and control me. I then do something really stupid, even destructive.

But God would say, "No, honey, your boyfriend left you because I have somebody better for you. I've got to get that loser out of your life. He's cheap anyway."

Thinking with my feelings brings death. Thinking with the promises of God brings life. When I think with my feelings, I make wrong choices, then I hurt so bad I start doing things to ease the pain. The things that I begin to do to ease the pain become a lifestyle. And once they become a lifestyle they become addictive. And once they become addictive, they become destructive. Now I've chosen death, when I could have chosen life.

When you choose life, everyone in your life is blessed. When you choose death, everyone in your life suffers.

Here's the deal.

Before you is placed life and death, which one will you choose? Sounds simple doesn't it? So why do so many people choose death?

Death comes in the form of:
- Addictions (substance abuse, gambling, eating, spending)
- Divorce
- Financial debt
- Cohabitating as though married, when not
- Immorality
- Etc.

Anything that goes against God's perfect will is choosing death. This choice is so crucial that God even gives the answer:

v.19 *So choose life in order that you may live, you and your descendants,*

Don't choose the things that are going to destroy you. Choose the things that bring you life.

What does it look like to "choose life?"

v.20 *by loving the LORD your God, by obeying His voice, and by holding fast to Him.*

I think of the poor woman in Matthew 9 who reached through the crowd and touched the hem of Jesus' garment. In that act, she was instantly healed. She set her sights on Jesus and would not let Him go.

Be careful that discouragement doesn't cause you to let God go. Hold fast to Him. Hold on to His Word and don't let it go. Don't go to the package store. Don't go to the night club. Don't go to the casino. Don't go to the mall or the convenience store. No. Go to God's Word. The best thing you can do is to sit down and let God's Word minister to you as you read it.

Conclusion;

v.21 *For this is your life and the length of your days, that you may live in the land which the LORD swore to your fathers, to Abraham, Isaac, and Jacob, to give them."*

This is where life comes from. These Scriptures outline who we are and how we are to live. It is also the basis for a full life.

This is our journey to wholeness.

1. We made a Decision To Turn Our Will and Life Over to the Care of God as We Understood Them. You have decided to turn your life over to God. Don't take it back. Once you've made that decision in your heart, it needs to be carried out in your life.

2. Choose wisely.

Do you remember the Indiana Jones movie, "The Last Crusade?" The story was about a search for the chalice that Jesus supposedly drank from. At the end of the movie, they finally found themselves in a secret room that was filled with chalices. When the bad guy entered the room he saw a multitude of chalices of all shapes and sizes. The danger was in drinking from the wrong chalice. He picked one that was beautifully decorated with precious jewels thinking this was a chalice worthy of God. When he drank from that chalice he turned to dust.

Indiana then entered the room and saw the same scene. A knight had been standing by watching the whole thing. Before Indiana Jones picked a chalice the knight said to him, "Choose wisely." He panned the room and saw off to the back, a simple wooden chalice.

He said, "This is the cup of a carpenter." He drank from the cup and found life. The point of the story is "Choose wisely." You can choose life or you can choose death.

God places before us the choice of life or death and then tells us to choose life and shows us what that looks like.

The rest is up to you.

Things I need to do

STEP 4

We Made A Searching And Fearless Moral Inventory Of Ourselves

STEP 4
We Made a Searching and Fearless Moral Inventory of Ourselves
Constructive Sorrow

This step has to do with honest introspection. This is one of the most important yet difficult things we have to do as believers who want to be overcomers. It's hard because it makes us take an honest look at ourselves and sometimes, we don't like what we see.

You would have to be perfect, like Jesus, to like what you see every time you look at yourself. This can be a difficult step because in it, we see our flaws and we don't like to see the flaws that we have. We may even find ourselves shunning them or denying them.

Have you ever noticed that what you don't like you shun?

- Food – something you do not like the taste or smell
- Person – someone who may have hurt you
- Place – somewhere that holds bad memories
- Chore – a job you have to do which you do not enjoy

• other ____________

That's because of our sinful, human nature. If I don't like it, I don't want it! But when it comes to honest introspection, that old way of thinking is dangerous to one's spiritual growth. It cannot be, "if I don't like it, then I don't want it." That will certainly hinder our growth.

Another word for this would be "Constructive Sorrow." Constructive sorrow means that when I take my inventory and I don't like what I see and it causes me sorrow, I can grow from it because it will be a constructive sorrow.

Sorrow comes in all fashions:

Loss of:

- Loved one
- Job
- Health

But there is another sorrow that we don't often consider. This is what we are going to find in Corinth. Let me take you back to first Century Greece. The Christians in the church in Corinth had gotten out of hand. An interesting thing about the Corinthian church. They excelled in spiritual gifts. They learned from the best teachers. Being situated on a peninsula that divided two bodies of water made it an overland shortcut for traders. In turn, they had a flourishing economy. And yet they were still babes in Christ; mere men. There were divisions among the people and disorders in their church services.

When this happens, we can't tell what is normal and what is not. A compulsive behavior may become the norm for an individual. Then, when the behavior is pointed out to that individual, the individual denies that there is a problem, because the "problem" has become the norm. The result is, abnormal becomes normal and dysfunction becomes normal.

The problem in the church was they became more focused on their tasks rather than their relationships. When people become more focused on tasks than on people, they are entering a dangerous place.

The important part of recovery is reconciliation with other people, without which long-term success is impossible. Paul said to the believers in Corinth that they needed to "shape up." He told them they were not honoring God.

Paul is going to refer to a previous letter of correction he wrote to these believers in Corinth.

II Corinthians 7:8 *For though I caused you sorrow by my letter, I do not regret it; though I did regret it--for I see that that letter caused you sorrow, though only for a while--*

No one likes to hear bad news, criticism or rebuke. Paul sent a letter of rebuke. Initially he was sorry that he hurt them. But after careful consideration, he realized that they needed to be rebuked and that would lead them to Godly sorrow. Remember, a Godly sorrow is a healthy sorrow that has been sent by God.

v.9 *I now rejoice, not that you were made sorrowful, but that you were made sorrowful to the point of repentance; for you were made sorrowful according to the will of God, so that you might not suffer loss in anything through us.*

Paul wasn't rejoicing because they were made sorrowful but because their sorrow would cause them to repent and change their ways.

To be sorrowful means distress or to be in heaviness. Have you ever had the feeling of a heavy heart? Did you ever feel that someone kicked you right in the heart by a rebuke they gave to you? What did you do with it?

The question is not, "Why do I feel the way I do?" The real question is, "What did I do with it?" Do you know what life is? Life is how I handle the experiences that come my way. Life is not the experiences, but rather, how I handle the experiences.

Like we saw in the last chapter, you can choose life or you can choose death. I've got a heavy heart. How will I handle it? Will I choose life or choose death? As God said, "Choose life so you will live, you and your descendants."

Paul said you were made sorrowful to the point of repentance. This is the purpose of sorrow. "Repentance" means a change of mind, to think differently. This is a change in thinking that results in a change in actions.

Their sorrow went in two ways:
1. to the point of repentance
2. according to the will of God
Here's how it worked:

God sent the sorrow through Paul's letter. The convicting power of the Holy Spirit caused them to feel sorrow for their behavior and they felt bad, which was the will of God for their lives.

We hear all the time, God wants you to feel good. God wants you to be happy. God wants you to be healthy. God wants you to be rich. God wants all your problems solved. Well, I don't know how true that is but I do know that at times, God wants you to feel bad. And that is because He wants you to be convicted about your bad behavior. He wants us all to feel so bad about our sinful behavior that we honestly look at ourselves and admit that we need to change. We say, I need to start thinking differently. I need to start doing things differently. I want to be on a road to recovery.

In my book, "Beauty in Darkness, Finding Hope In Distressing Times" there is a chapter entitled, "Why Pain?" This is one of the most commonly asked questions in humanity. Why is there pain in my life?

Part of the purpose of pain is God chipping away the parts of you that hinder your spiritual growth so you can shine for Him. God is shaping, molding, chipping and hammering us into the image of Christ. No doubt about it, this process can be painful.

When you rebel against the pain, you are hindering the work God is doing in your life.

Recommendations

1. If you have the book, read it (again).

2. If you don't have it, get it. (and read it).

(order it at www.inspiringbooks.org)

v.10 *For the sorrow that is according to the will of God produces a repentance <u>without regret</u>, leading to salvation, but the sorrow of the world produces death.*

I think of two individuals in the New Testament, The Apostle Peter and Judas Iscariot. Peter denied he knew the Lord and Judas betrayed Him for 30 pieces of silver, the price of a slave. Peter's sorrow produced a repentance and he was restored back to Jesus. Judas' sorrow was filled with regret and he, instead, hanged himself for what he had done. Judas chose death but Peter chose life.

For the sorrow that is according to the will of God produces a repentance <u>without regret</u>, leading to salvation...

Salvation here is a reference, not to being "born again through faith in Christ" but a literal deliverance. This is what this book is about. It is about deliverance from compulsive behaviors.

Therefore, pain from introspection brings constructive sorrow. So don't be afraid of the pain. Don't be afraid of the hurt. It is all part of the process. Don't condemn yourself. Don't run from it. Don't deny it and don't shun it. Rather, embrace it because it came from God. God sent it to get you going in a different direction because the direction you were going in was destructive. This sorrow is to instill a repentance that is without regret because corrections are being made. The result is deliverance and a place of safety. This is learning from our mistakes. We can now look back and say, "That was hard but it made me a better person." If we don't get to the place of safety by thinking differently, we remain in a place of danger.

v.11 *For behold* – look at that!

what earnestness this very thing, this godly sorrow, has produced in you:

Paul is getting them to see the good side. I know you felt bad. I know that letter hurt you. But it was intended to set you straight. But look at how you are getting on fire for God again. You're being delivered from your old ways.

The "earnestness" Paul is speaking about is eagerness. Their eagerness has returned. It is so easy, without even realizing it, to lose one's eagerness for God. Then, you wake up one day and you find yourself far from Him.

Beach Illustration.

As a child you may have gone to the beach and played out in the waves of the ocean. Before going into the water your parents said, "Now don't go out too far and keep an eye on where you are." After about an hour or two of playing in the water you look up at the beach and everything looks different. You can't see your umbrella. What happened? Without even realizing it, you slowly drifted away. The current was so subtle, you didn't realize that it was taking you away.

This can happen to us spiritually. It happens when your Christian walk becomes a routine. A routine makes something hard. Jesus told a parable about seed that fell on a road. The road was actually a path in the garden made by the routine of walking on it day after day. The ground became so hard that it could not receive the seed and the birds came and ate them up. Matthew 13. Routine hardens the heart. When you find yourself in a spiritual routine, it's time to break up that ground. Sometimes that is a painful process.

v.11 *What vindication of yourselves, what indignation, what fear, what longing, what zeal, what avenging of wrong! In everything you demonstrated yourselves to be innocent in the matter.*

Vindication is a crying out to God. Indignation is blaming yourself for drifting away. It is not about blaming others for where I am. Paul speaks about having a healthy fear for drifting away from God. All of these working together bring us back to God! It has become a lesson learned. The hard lessons are the best lessons to learn. We never forget them.

Jeremiah the Old Testament prophet said in

Lamentations 3:32 *For if He causes grief, then He will have compassion according to His abundant loving-kindness.*

Wow. God causes grief. Any good parent will give their child grief when they place themselves in a dangerous situation. But then He offers compassion to those who respond.

This is what causes people to slip into compulsive behaviors. They begin with a bad behavior or putting themselves in a dangerous situation. When they get grief and pain, they blame everybody else and make themselves the victim. They then try to dull the pain with some type of behavior. The behavior is usually a destructive behavior. They want to take their mind off of themselves. This is why Step 4 is getting your mind back on yourself. It's okay to look at yourself.

Who doesn't look at themselves every day in a natural sense? We look into the mirror before leaving the house and make any necessary changes or adjustments before going out.

Spiritually, we look into the mirror of the Word of God and perform a similar duty. The Apostle Paul tells us to "*Examine ourselves, to see if we are in the faith.*" {II Corinthians 13:5}

God doesn't leave you guilty or sorrowful. He has all the compassion that you need to keep going forward.

Summary:

1. We all have to deal with sorrow; You can stuff it down or ignore it; you can try to drown it out but it won't go away. We need to accept it and let it be part of our process. Use it as a motivation to search your soul. Things do not go away that we ignore.

2. Not all sorrow is bad; there is a Godly sorrow {sorrow sent by God) that leads to repentance.

3. Sorrow hurts, for a time. But when you are honest and understand why you have it you will find deliverance. It is not a permanent sorrow. It is meant to get you moving again.

4. Never regret or turn from the pain God sends into your life. It has its purpose. God knows what He is doing in your life. You can either get with God's program or continue in compulsive behaviors.

5. You have the choice;

a.   Morbid, self-condemnation {Judas}.

b.   Honest, self-evaluation {Peter}.

Don't think, "Not me. How can there be anything wrong with me?" That is why God sent the pain.

Accept your sorrow as a positive part of your recovery, not as a punishment.

I'd like to leave you with the words of Isaiah.

Isaiah 1:16-18 *Wash yourselves, make yourselves clean; Remove the evil of your deeds from My sight. Cease to do evil,*

Learn to do good; Seek justice, Reprove the ruthless, Defend the orphan, Plead for the widow.

"Come now, and let us reason together," Says the LORD, "Though your sins are as scarlet, They will be as white as snow; Though they are red like crimson, They will be like wool.

"If you consent and obey, You will eat the best of the land;

"But if you refuse and rebel, You will be devoured by the sword." Truly, the mouth of the LORD has spoken.

Things I need to do

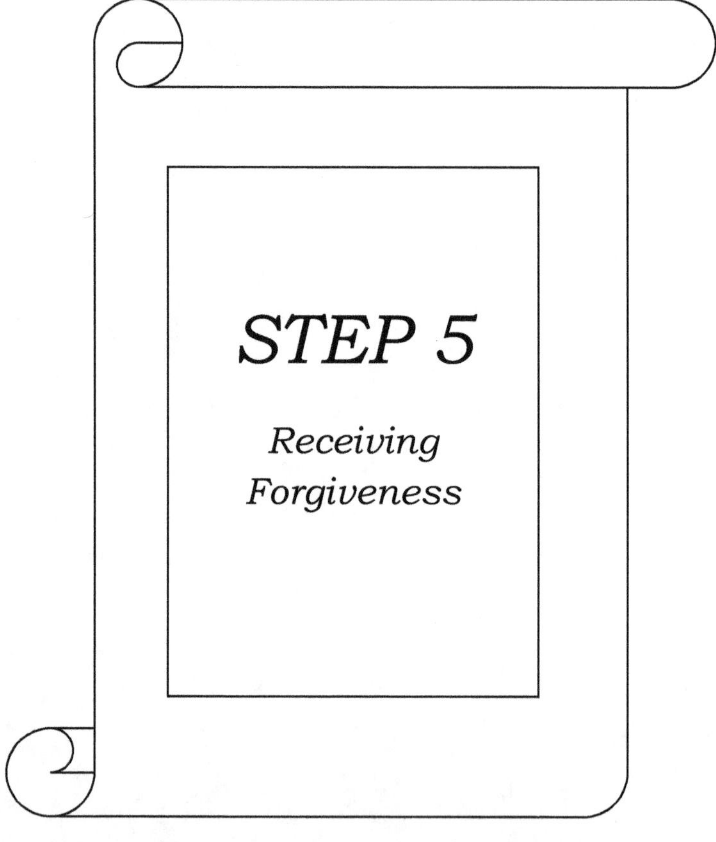
STEP 5
Receiving
Forgiveness

Step 5
Receiving Forgiveness

Review

Step 4: "We Made A Searching and Fearless Moral Inventory of Ourselves." We said not all sorrow is bad.

There is a Godly sorrow that leads to repentance. That Godly sorrow is conviction. It is God showing us where we are wrong. We feel broken about that but it brings us to a change of mind, a change of heart. Sorrow does hurt for a time but when you use it for the reason for which it was sent, you find deliverance. Godly sorrow is not punishment, it is meant for deliverance. Never regret or turn from the pain that God sends into your life. It has a purpose.

When this pain comes, you have a choice. You can enter into morbid, self-condemnation or honest, self-evaluation. Though honest, self-evaluation seems to be the better choice, morbid, self-condemnation seems to be the practice.

And don't think, "Not me. How can there be anything wrong with me?" That is why God sent the pain. If there is any pain from Godly conviction, God sent the pain because there is something He wants you to see.

So accept your Godly sorrow as a positive part of your recovery, not as a punishment.

Accepting the truth about ourselves is a big part of our spiritual growth and recovery. And when it comes to forgiveness, we often have the wrong attitude.

Many people feel the forgiveness they need has to be earned. We cannot undo what has been done. But we can go on from it. Too many people don't understand that forgiveness is from the grace of God. God's grace is His treatment toward us. It is unmerited and undeserved. It is His graciousness toward us, not because of who we are, but because of who He is.

You have probably also noticed, it is often easier for some people to give forgiveness than to receive it for themselves. Forgiveness goes both ways. It goes out from you and it comes to you. You must be on the receiving and the giving end of forgiveness. If you don't learn to receive forgiveness from God, you will end up punishing yourself in lieu of receiving forgiveness. This opens the door to compulsive behaviors.

Background:
Saul of Tarsus was a man in need of much forgiveness. His zeal for God was so great that he perceived the new Christian movement as a threat to his Jewish religion. He was committed to stamping out the movement.

Judaism was around for a number of centuries and it seemed to be working fine for everybody. Then a new wave of belief arrived on the scene. This Jesus of Nazareth came preaching forgiveness through belief in Him as the Messiah and the shedding of His own blood on a Roman cross. In doing so, He introduced the grace of God. People began to be attracted to that message of grace. They were hearing that God will accept them the way they are and that God loves them as they are. And if they are willing to believe in Jesus and give their lives to Him, He will work in their lives and will change them from the inside out. He will also guarantee them a place in His eternal kingdom. That was a wonderful message but the religious people didn't like the message because it took people away from their religious rituals and observances. It took them away from formality. It also conflicted with their works program to gain acceptance with God.

Saul of Tarsus was a Pharisee of the highest rank. He committed himself to stamping out this new movement called Christianity.

Notice Paul's commentary.

Acts 26:10 *And this is just what I did in Jerusalem; not only did I lock up many of the saints in prisons, having received authority from the chief priests, but also when they were being put to death I cast my vote against them.*

v.11 *And as I punished them often in all the synagogues, I tried to force them to blaspheme; and being furiously enraged at them, I kept pursuing them even to foreign cities.*

Paul went out of his way from city to city trying to get people to deny this Jesus of Nazareth. Now that is zeal! When you go out of your way to hurt somebody, that's zeal. It is bad enough to hurt people when they are in your way. But when you go "out of your way" to hurt them, that's zeal.

It's interesting. The bad things we do never seem that bad, until we discover Jesus Christ in our lives. Perhaps this is one of the tests of true conversion. When Christ comes into your life, it is like someone washed the window. Now you can see in a way you never saw before.

Hopefully, there are things in your life that you used to do before Christ that you would never do now that you have Him. (He has you.)

This include:

- things we do
- places we go
- words we say

Why this change? It is not because you are better than somebody else. The change is because those things are not satisfying anymore. They don't get it done. The things I used to do to find fulfillment don't fulfill me anymore, because I have the Spirit of God now and a new nature. Those places I used to go, I no longer go, for the same reason. And so it is with some of the things I used to say.

When the Spirit of God comes inside of a person, something happens to that person and things begin to change. Something happened to Saul of Tarsus and he became Paul the Apostle.

So here is Paul the Apostle. He is standing before King Agrippa answering for the crime of preaching the gospel of Jesus Christ. Paul got arrested for the very thing he was arresting people for. What happened was,

Paul did meet this Jesus of Nazareth, himself, and Paul became a believer and follower of Christ.

Paul became a new man through "forgiveness." You see, forgiveness changes everything!

Perhaps this is why so many people are afraid of God because they are afraid of being forgiven. If they become forgiven, it means they can't punish themselves any longer. They think, "If I am forgiven, I can't hurt myself any longer. But I want to hurt myself because I am guilty. And I need to punish myself to make things right."

God is saying, "No, I punished Jesus for you. Things have already been made right. Just receive the forgiveness that I have for you."

As Paul stood before King Agrippa for preaching the Gospel, he spoke about his strict Jewish training. From a child, he learned his lessons and became a chief Pharisee. He obeyed the Law as well as anyone could. Any Jewish mother would look at Saul of Tarsus, the Pharisee, and say to her little boy, "Do you see Saul? I want you to grow up and become just like him." He had become very religious and he kept the Law. But he wasn't saved, he was just religious.

It's amazing the amount of persecution that is done in the name of religion. Here he is, going from city to city persecuting Christians, in the name of God! There have been wars in just about every century, in the name of God. How does that happen when God is a God of Peace? That is why religion doesn't get it done. It is only through a personal relationship with Jesus Christ that things can change. Jesus didn't die so we could be religious. He died so we could have a one on one relationship with Him. He wants us to do life with Him.

Now, Paul begins to share his testimony. A person's testimony of what God has done in their life can be the best witness, even over Bible knowledge.

And he shares his testimony with boldness. His testimony speaks of the change that came into his life after meeting Jesus Christ. He explained that he was routing our Christians by the authority of the chief priest. He used the words "breathing out threats and murder against the Lord's disciples." Paul attained letters giving him authority to round up Christians, arrest them and execute them. They were called members of the Way.

Then something happened to him. As he was traveling at midday, a light shined upon him and his travelling companions brighter than the sun. It was like a giant flashbulb went off or a burst of lightning. It actually blinded him and knocked him off of his horse.

Then, God said something that only Saul could hear. When Paul gave this testimony another time in Acts 22, he said the other men who were with him saw the light but did not understand the words that were being spoken.

Hopefully, it is not like that with you. You hear, but fail to understand. You don't allow it to go deep within your heart. Paul continued.

He explained that when he fell to the ground, he heard a voice say to him, Saul, Saul, why are you persecuting Me? It is hard to kick against the goads.

A goad is a sharp stick used to prod an ox. If he kicks against it, he brings further pain to himself. It is also used to steer the animal to go where the shepherd wants him to go. Paul is kicking against the leading of God.

When God tries to steer you in your own life and you kick against that, it brings pain. Then you enter into a compulsive behavior to ease the pain.

At this point, Paul recognized that it was Jesus who he was really persuting.

Now, this is the turning point of Saul's life. Saul knew God but now he knows Jesus Christ.

Here is what Paul is learning. If I am persecuting Christ, I am persecuting God. If I am persecuting the people of Christ, I am persecuting Christ and therefore, persecuting God. The way we treat God's people, well, He takes it personally.

Saul is at a spiritual crossroads where he has to make a decision.

The voice told him to get up on his feet. "Get up and stand on your feet" means that he is forgiven. I've watched your life Saul, I've seen what you've done. And I want you to know that I have a future for you. You are forgiven so you can live in that future. Will you accept it? And that question goes to each one of us as well. Will you accept God's forgiveness and accept the future He has for you?

Forgiveness gets you out of the rut that you've been living in. It is where you feel you have done a lot of damage, no one likes you. Forgiveness does away with all of that. Forgiveness says you have great value, you do matter. That is why we have to receive the forgiveness that God offers.

A similar scene is found in Matthew 9. Jesus came into a city and they brought to him a man who couldn't walk. Jesus said to him, "Your sins are forgiven." Boy did the scribes get angry! They were religious, just like Saul of Tarsus was.

Jesus said to them, "What is easier to say, your sins are forgiven or get up and walk?" Then He said; "So you will know that I have the authority to forgive sins, I said get up and go home." Jesus demonstrated that He had authority to forgive sins because He did the hard thing. He worked a miracle and healed the man. The healing proved that He was God.

If you are down because of guilt, God's word for you is "get up" and start moving. Forgiveness is available and the cross has made it possible.

Back to Saul:

Christ told Saul that He had big pans for him. He would use Paul's testimony for His glory. This is why some of the worst people before salvation become some of the best witnesses for Christ. Sometimes people who were always "good" have a difficult time seeing their need for a Savior. Yet, everyone has failure and a need for forgiveness. The difference between what you were and what you are is Christ.

Saul of Tarsus was a changed life just like any one of us can be a changed life. And the reason he was a changed life was because he received forgiveness.

It is in receiving forgiveness and going on in God's purpose that you are restored.

There are two important aspects of your testimony:

1. It is an admission of your sins which usher in forgiveness.

2. Your testimony of what God has done is freeing to others who are bound in sin and guilt.

Your testimony makes some think, "Wow, God did that for you? I wonder if He can do that for me. Do you think God would forgive me the way He forgave you?" The answer is, Of course He will.

Israel constantly rebelled against God. Yet, God created Israel for His purposes.

God delivered them from Egypt.

1. He gave them the promises of a new land that flowed with milk and honey.

2. He gave them victory in battles. And yet, they constantly turned to worship false gods. In spite of their rebellions, God's heart toward Israel is revealed through the prophet, Hosea.

How can I give you up, O Ephraim? How can I surrender you, O Israel?... My heart is turned over within Me, all My compassions are kindled. Hosea 11:8

We have to see God this way because this is the way He is.

The LORD is compassionate and gracious, slow to anger and abounding in loving-kindness. Psalm 103:8

Forgiveness always brings hope and purpose.

Yes, your sin may be great but God's forgiveness is greater. No one is so bad that they can't be forgiven. God's grace is greater.

He said;

1. to the paralytic – get up and go home

2. to the woman caught in adultery – neither do I condemn you

3. to Saul of Tarsus – get up and stand on your feet

4. to you - *the loving-kindness of the LORD is from everlasting to everlasting on those who fear Him,* Psalm 103:17

The Law was given to show us our sins.

But where sin increased, grace abounded all the more, Rom 5:20

so that, as sin reigned in death, even so grace would reign through righteousness to eternal life through Jesus Christ our Lord. Rom 5:21

Picture a little fish. He is the only one swimming in the Amazon River. You say to the little fish, Drink up little fish, drink up. There is more than you need. That's forgiveness.

Things I need to do

STEP 6

I Am Ready To
Have God Remove
My Character
Defects

STEP 6
I Am Ready To Have God Remove My
Character Defects
Discovering Hope

You have now arrived at a place where you are forgiven and accepted by God. He has lifted you up and planted you on firm ground. He commands you to go forward with your life. Arriving at Step 6, we are ready to have God remove the defects of our character.

Our character defects are the misfiring's in our thinking that no one knows is going on but us. This is our private world. Only you and God know what goes on in your private world.

Removing character defects does not mean you are going to attain perfection. No one can do that. But remember that we are on a journey to wholeness. This simply means that I am getting control of my life back. I am beginning to be set free from compulsive behaviors.

In this story before us, we will see how easy it is to get stuck in a rut, in a routine and just settle there with no hope of better things. A routine can be dangerous when it is a routine that leads to a dead end and you believe this is the way it's supposed to be.

The Story

Jesus went down to this large, public pool and let's see what happened.

John 5:2 *Now there is in Jerusalem by the sheep gate a pool, which is called in Hebrew Bethesda, having five porches.*

v.3 *In these lay a multitude of those who were sick, blind, lame, and withered, [waiting for the moving of the waters;*

v.4 *[for an angel of the Lord went down at certain seasons into the pool and stirred up the water; whoever then first, after the stirring up of the water, stepped in was made well from whatever disease with which he was afflicted.]*

Note;

The bracketed information is not found in the earliest manuscripts. Therefore, commentators regard it as "spurious," or doubtful/questionable.

Others say this was the ministry of angels to do this thing.

Whatever the case, the point is not if the waters were troubled and people were healed. Rather, the point is that this man was in a condition for years and had grown accustomed to it. He was in a bad place and he accepted the fact that he would just live there in that place for the rest of his life. He had no hope, no help and no future.

John 5:5 *A man was there who had been ill for thirty-eight years.*

That's a long time to live with an affliction. This was at least half of his life, if not most of his life.

Jesus asked a legitimate question.

v.6 When Jesus saw him lying there, and knew that he had already been a long time in that condition, He said to him, "Do you wish to get well?"

v.7 The sick man answered Him, "Sir, I have no man to put me into the pool when the water is stirred up, but while I am coming, another steps down before me."

Why did Jesus ask this question? Wasn't it obvious that the man was in need? After all, these people were not there because they liked swimming in public swimming pools. They were not there to work on their tans. They were there because they believed that at certain times the water became stirred up by an angel and the first one in the pool received a healing.

The question Jesus asked seemed rather obvious. "Do you want to get well?" That's like going to the hospital today and asking a patient, "Do you want to get well?"

Actually, after 38 years, it may have been that the man's hope had died. When you have no hope, you become content with where you are, as bad as that might be. How many people do you think there are in the world today who have no hope for their present condition? So they stay in it. They live in it. They do absolutely nothing to break out of it.

You may even think to yourself, "Why do they put up with that? Why don't they break out?" The answer is because they have no hope. Hope is the fuel that keeps the engine running. If there is no hope there is no fuel, and therefore, nothing happens. That's where this man was. As bad as his situation was he became content with it.

What kind of people today feel there is no hope for them? Perhaps those who remain in their addiction or those in an abusive relationship. They have no hope so they don't think they can break out.

Everyone must ask themselves, "Do I really want to be healed?" or "Do I just want continue in my affliction?"

Did the man by the pool answer the Lord's question? NO! He did not answer the question.

There can be two understandings to his answer, "I have no one to put me into the pool."

1.	I have no friends to help me.

2.	I'm not really facing my issue. I'm not really looking at my problem. When you are not looking at your problem, you are then looking at everybody else. People that never get victory over their problem are the people that never look at their problem. They look at everybody else instead of what's going on inside of them. This was true of this man because he didn't answer the question, "Do you want to get well?"

He could have said, "Yes, I wish to get well."

True, he had no friends. All of the others that were there had their own issues. They were probably jockeying for position to get into the pool themselves.

Sick people can't help sick people. Someone that is struggling cannot help someone that is struggling. A drowning person cannot save a drowning person. A person struggling with a compulsive behavior cannot help a person struggling with a compulsive behavior. When you are struggling, or drowning or have a compulsive behavior, you are not concerned with other people. Perhaps sick people won't help sick people because they are consumed with their own situation.

This man put his trust in people but they couldn't help him and they wouldn't help him. So, there he sat. Year after year, year after year, there he sat. How easy it is to do that. If I can't get the help I need from people then I will just stay where I am. Can you see how easy it is to stay where you are if you have the wrong perspective? There comes a time in a person's life when you have to stop looking to other people. There comes a time when you have to take your own personal responsibility and do the thing that needs to be done.

This man is going to learn a valuable lesson. And the lesson is, sometimes only Jesus Christ can bring the release you are looking for. So there has to be seriousness about going to God. Many folks go to God haphazardly, passively, but they don't go after God with all their heart, soul, mind and strength. You have to go after God believing that He is the only One who can get you out of this program, out of this system, out of this pattern. Only Christ can deliver you.

Jesus is a friend to the friendless. This man didn't have a friend in the world and Jesus comes along and says, "I'll be your friend."

You see, no one has to be totally friendless. Christ will always come by and He will stand by you. He will be a friend to you.

And to make matters worse, the man continues to make excuses. First, he said there is no one to put me in the pool. Then he says, *while I am coming, another steps down before me.* His eyes are on what other people are doing rather than himself.

Sometimes, we find ourselves in a bad place where it's easy to blame other people for the choices we've made. We have to remember that we are responsible for the choices that we make. Sometimes we make good choices and sometimes we make choices that put us in a bad place. But the whole point of this teaching is God can deliver you.

We are going to see that not only is his body lame but his attitude is lame. And isn't that the basis of compulsive behaviors? Notice what Jesus said.

v.8 *Jesus said to him, "Get up, pick up your pallet and walk."*

There are some things that only God can do but we must cooperate by faith. If we don't act on what God is saying, there is no benefit. God gives the direction but we have to step out. And we have to get it done.

Jesus gives him 3 things to do:
1. "Get up" off the ground
2. "Pick up" your bed
3. "Walk" away

Jesus didn't enter into a discussion with the man. He didn't ask him what he was comfortable with. He simply commanded him to get up. There are some things God tells us to do and He says to do it now. That's because if you don't do it now, you never will. Instead, excuses will begin to fly and the result is, ten years from now, you will still be in the same place, making the same excuses.

The result of faith:

v.9 *Immediately the man became well, and picked up his pallet and began to walk.*

What was it that allowed this man to be healed by Christ?

1. He let Christ be real with him:

"Do you want to get well?" This required a time of introspection. He had to ask himself, "Do I really want to continue to live like this or do I want to break out?" Jesus made him get real and face the issue.

We ask the question again, "Do I really want to get well?" No one gets well by accident. You have to do the required thing.

2. He had to stop making excuses.

"He had no one to put him into the water." Jesus wants him to know it's not about other people. It's about your heart. What do you think about you? Forget them. They're not going to live your life. Only you can live your life. So what is going on inside of you? Stop making excuses for where you are. Don't say you have no one to help you. You have God to help you. God can help any person in any situation.

3. He listened to Christ and believed Him.

"He picked up his pallet and began to walk."

This was all the work of God but it took honesty, trust and obedience to make it happen.

Now, think about this in your own condition. Is there something in your life that has control? What is that behavior you are trying to overcome?

Three questions:

1. Do you really want to be made well?

2. Are you ready to stop making excuses?

3. Will you do your part, believe and obey?

If so, God can and will remove your character defects. He will do His part but you must do your part. If not, things will never improve.

Closing thought:

If things don't improve, they will only get worse. You see, life is moving, it is not stagnant. You are either moving forward or you are moving backwards. Your life is either getting better or it is getting worse. There is movement to life. Which way is your life moving?

Things I need to do

STEP 7

We Humbly Ask
God To Remove
Our Shortcomings

STEP 7
We Humbly Ask God To Remove
Our Shortcomings
Honest Before God

Wanting to better oneself is a noble thing. Most people, if not all people, need a victory in some area of their life.

When a compulsive behavior dominates one's life, some serious changes are needed.

This step has to do with "attitude." This is why you have to listen in all humility. You have to really be personal with God. When we talk about attitude, we are talking about the place that is deep inside of you. It's the inside world where we live. Only we and God can arrest that area.

Attitude is our manner of acting, feeling or thinking. Body language can express attitude. Facial expressions can express attitude.

Everyone has an attitude because everyone acts, feels and thinks. It is often our attitude that gets us into trouble. That's because it leads us to actions and those actions can become compulsive behaviors. That behavior begins to dominate me. Now I can't resist. And there are triggers in my life that push me into that behavior. Maybe it's something that gets you angry. Maybe it's somebody's name. Maybe it's a certain word someone says to you. Whatever that button is that somebody pushes, it gets you into that compulsive behavior. But if we trace it all the way back to the beginning, it starts with an attitude.

In this chapter we will learn how to overcome our shortcomings by changing our attitude. It is all about the way that we think in our little invisible world.

A big part of our attitudes is PRIDE. Pride is the driving force behind everything we do wrong. Pride is the driving force behind the things that we say that we shouldn't.

Because of our pride we:
- Hide
- Become defensive
- Make excuses
- Have delusions of superiority

Pride always makes us feel higher than we really are and many times, above other people as well. These are all the results of our sin nature. We are all born with a corrupt, sin nature. And if we feed that sin nature, it gets stronger and stronger. We then act in that nature and pride is at the helm.

When you become a Christian, you receive a divine nature. The divine nature is the Spirit of God. If you feed that divine nature, you become more like Christ and you have victory over the sin nature. Which nature is going to win is determined by which nature you feed. If you feed your flesh, your flesh will rule. If you feed your spirit, your spirit will rule. You can feed your flesh on the pods of the world like the Prodigal Son did. (Luke 15:11) Or you can feed your spirit on the Word of God and watch things begin to change like you could never imagine. *(See my book, "The Loving Father And The Lost Son" at www.inspiringbooks.org).*

Think of Adam and Eve in the garden. They did well for a while until they fell into sin. After the fall, they discovered that they were naked so they tried to cover themselves and hide from God. That's what pride causes us to do – run away and hide. Sometimes compulsive behaviors are a way of running away and hiding. Let me hide in this activity. You may think you are hiding but you are not. When Adam and Eve put on fig leaves and hid behind a tree, they really thought God couldn't find them. They thought they were hiding but He knew where they were.

When you hide in a compulsive behavior, you are only hiding from yourself. Everyone else sees you but pride makes you think that you're hiding. You need some drastic changes in your life. That begins with changing your attitude. Those of us who have tried to protect ourselves this way need a dramatic change in attitude.

Now, when drastic measures like this have to be taken, it's good to have a pattern or a model to look at. Jesus Christ can be that model to show us how to have the right attitude in life.

Philippians 2:5 *Have this attitude in yourselves which was also in Christ Jesus,*

There's the model. What was in that little world inside of Jesus? Let that same thought process be inside of you.

v.6 *who, although He existed in the form of God, did not regard equality with God a thing to be grasped,*

v.7 *but emptied Himself, taking the form of a bond-servant, and being made in the likeness of men.*

v.8 *Being found in appearance as a man, He humbled Himself by becoming obedient to the point of death, even death on a cross.*

Here is what I love about the Bible. The things it tells us to do, can be done. If not, it wouldn't tell us.

Contemporary English Version says; "Think the same way Christ Jesus thought..."

By reading through the Gospels, you can see Jesus in action and witness how He thought by the things that He did.

As a man, Jesus sought to promote the glory of God. This was His attitude in life. Jesus never made life about Himself. He always made it about His Father. That is so freeing. When we make life about us, we can easily become disappointed. God will not allow us to have a fulfilled life if we make life about us. Life doesn't work that way. God says to make it about Him and we will be fulfilled.

v.6 Tells us this is so;

Who, although He existed in the <u>form</u> of God, did not regard equality with God a thing to be grasped,

The word "form" *morphe* means nature, shape, form. It is a reference to the deity of Christ. What was in God was in Jesus. They had the same nature.

Colossians 1:15 *He is the <u>image</u> of the invisible God, the firstborn of all creation.*

The word "image" *eikon* means likeness, representation, resemblance (another ref. to His deity).

So, although Jesus pre-existed in the form of God because He is God,

v.6 (He) did not regard equality with God a thing to be <u>*grasped*</u>*,*

The word "grasped" means robbery. He did not see His equality with God to be robbery. He did not take what was not His. Robbery is taking something that doesn't belong to you. Deity belonged to Him. So what did He do instead?

In eternity past He was God. He was physically born into the human race and lived for thirty-three years.

v.7 but <u>*emptied*</u> *Himself, taking the form of a bond-servant, and being made in the likeness of men.*

The word "emptied" means that He laid aside His deity. He limited Himself to the human experience. He did not parade Himself around as God and use His divine power for His own benefit. Jesus only used His divine power for the benefit of others. Living in the human limitation qualified Him to be our pattern, our role model.

Instead;

v.8 Being found in appearance as a man, He humbled Himself by <u>*becoming obedient*</u> *to the point of death, even death on a cross.*

You would think that being a man (human) the natural response would be to humble oneself. But most of us humans have failed to humble ourselves. Note the depth of His humility.

He humbled Himself "by becoming obedient." Obedience is a form of humility. Rebellion or disobedience is a form of pride. Jesus said "If you do the things that I command you, you are my friends." That's humility.

Another important truth is that God gives grace to the humble but resists the proud. James 4:6

How far did this humility stretch?

v.8 *to the point of death.*

He was humble until there was nothing left.

Ask yourself, "Is this the kind of Christianity I want to be involved in?" If not, there is no other form of Christianity. That's because Jesus is our pattern, our model.

Notice the kind of death.

even death on a cross. – the worst kind of death!

Jesus not only obeyed God but He also died the worst kind of death. He is demonstrating true humility.

We have a contrast between rebellion from pride and obedience through humility. If I live in rebellion and pride, I live physically but I die spiritually. If I live in humility and obedience, I may die physically but I live spiritually. So which one do I want to live in?

Jesus said, "If you do the things that I command you, you'll be My friends." You'll be like Me.

Winners hang with winners and losers hang with losers.

What do you want to become? You will become what you surround yourself with.

God rewarded Him.

v.9 *For this reason also, God highly exalted Him, and bestowed on Him the name which is above every name.*

Jesus had the highest rank that could bestowed upon a human being. He is at the top of humanity.

Notice the contrast. This is Jesus in His humility. The Old Testament prophet, Isaiah, prophesied this would happen to Jesus.

Isaiah 50:6 *I gave My back to those who strike Me, and My cheeks to those who pluck out the beard; I did not cover My face from humiliation and spitting.*

Isaiah 53:3 *He was despised and forsaken of men, a man of sorrows and acquainted with grief; and like one from whom men hide their face He was despised, and we did not esteem Him.*

These Scriptures prophesied about the humility of Jesus Christ when He came. He would allow His beard to be plucked out. He would offer His face to be punched and beaten. People would despise Him.

Have you ever been around people who despised you? You can feel it. You can feel it when they're talking about you and when you're not welcome in their circle. You feel like you're alone in the world. That's how Jesus felt.

He was despised by His own people. He created them. And He accepted it. He accepted it all. They didn't honor Him nor did they value Him. At His birth there was no room in the inn.

At the end of His earthly life, before He went to the cross, He went to the garden of Gethsemane.

Matthew 26:39 *He fell on His face and prayed, saying, "My Father, if it is possible, let this cup pass from Me; yet not as I will, but as You will."*

Father, My desire is not to do this but whatever is Your desire, that is what I will do.

Think about that thing you're trying to get the victory over. Think about that sin, that pattern. The path to victory is not to live in your will but in God's will. May the attitude that was in Christ be the same attitude in you.

Jesus received strength from obeying His Father.

John 4:34 *My food is to do the will of Him who sent Me and to accomplish His work.*

He understood His mission.

John 6:38 *For I have come down from heaven, not to do My own will, but the will of Him who sent Me.*

Jesus is God but He still does not carry out His own will. Why couldn't He do His will if He is God? He is our pattern. He is showing us how a human being is supposed to live. A human is to seek out the will of God and do the will of God. Realize that everything I want to do is going to destroy me because it comes from a corrupt mind. But the things that God would have me to do are the things that are going to fulfill me.

II Corinthians 8:9 *though He was rich, yet for your sake He became poor, so that you through His poverty might become rich.*

He left heaven and grew up in Nazareth.

Now, in His reward, the psalmist prophesied about His future.

Psalm 72:11 *And let all kings bow down before him, All nations serve him.*

Revelation 19:16 *And on His robe and on His thigh He has a name written, "KING OF KINGS, AND LORD OF LORDS."*

Philippians 2:9 *God highly exalted Him, and bestowed on Him the name which is above every name,*

He was lowered down to the dirt but God exalted Him. There is a reward for the attitude of humility.

Application:

Hebrews 12:2 *fixing our eyes on Jesus, the author and perfecter* (completer) *of faith,* (Study Him as your role model).

v.3 *consider Him who has endured such hostility by sinners against Himself, so that you will not grow weary and lose heart.* (Think about all that He went through).

A sad place to be in life is where you lose heart. You've run out of gas. You only want to sleep. *Hope delayed makes the heart sick.* Proverbs 13:12

When you look at Jesus, you can only become humbled. For who can stand, comparing their works to His? Who can look at the life of Christ and not be humbled about their own life?

When Jesus was nailed to the cross He said, *"Father, forgive them. They do not know what they are doing."* Luke 23:34 When someone passes you on the right on the highway, you pray, "Father, give them a flat!"

If you are serious about recovering lost ground, do these three things:

Action Point.
1. Look and keep looking at Jesus.
   (study Jesus)
2. Let humility begin to work in you.
   (take the lower seat)
3. Ask God to change your attitude in areas where it is prideful.
   (be honest before God)

The places I am prideful are where I:
- Hide
- Defend myself
- Make excuses
- Blame others
- Feel superior
- ______________

Never compare yourself to another person. Be honest before God and He will remove your shortcomings.

Things I need to do

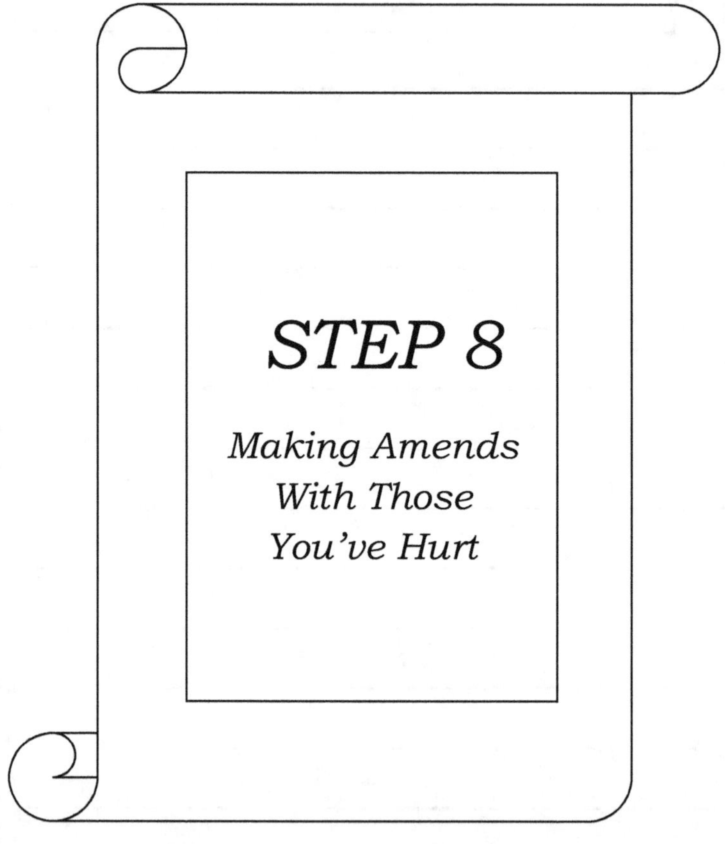
STEP 8

Making Amends
With Those
You've Hurt

STEP 8
Making Amends With Those You've Hurt
Making Amends

Our God is a God of balance. He is also a God of practicality.

Therefore, because He is "our" God, He wants us to be balanced and practical in our lives as well. If not, dysfunction reigns in your life and then in your family and wherever else you may take yourself.

One of the ways we can maintain balance and practicality in our lives is by making amends with those we've hurt.

In Exodus 22, God gave the principle of restitution. "Restitution" means to restore or make good for damage caused.

> v.10 *If a man gives his neighbor a donkey, an ox, a sheep, or any animal to keep for him, and it dies or is hurt or is driven away while no one is looking,*

> v.11 *an oath before the LORD shall be made by the two of them that he has not laid hands on his neighbor's property; and its owner shall accept it, and he shall not make restitution.*

> v.12 *But if it is actually stolen from him, he shall make restitution to its owner.*
>
> v.13 *If it is all torn to pieces, let him bring it as evidence; he shall not make restitution for what has been torn to pieces.*
>
> v.14 *If a man borrows anything from his neighbor, and it is injured or dies while its owner is not with it, he shall make full restitution.*

What we have here in these verses is what I call unintentional loss and negligent loss.

Unintentional loss:

v.10 The animal is put in the safe keeping of someone but the animal disappears and no one saw it. The man in charge swears that he knows nothing of what happened. He is released from any damages.

Negligent loss: (intentional loss)

v.12 It is assumed he is watching the animal along with his own flock or herd. His friend's animal was taken but not his own. That would arouse suspicion of fraud.

In this case, the man must make restitution. Point being, there are areas of somebody's life where neglect causes loss.

Or;

> v.13 *If it is all torn to pieces, let him bring it as evidence; he shall not make restitution for what has been torn to pieces.*

If a loss occurs, the animal is destroyed and no one has it, that person is released from restitution.

The reason God gave these laws is to keep people's lives balanced and practical. Honesty is also a part of that practicality. This stops people from taking advantage of other people.

Intentional loss: (negligent)

v.14 *If a man borrows anything from his neighbor, and it is injured or dies while its owner is not with it, he shall make full restitution.*

God is teaching the virtue of personal responsibility. We are speaking in this chapter about taking responsibility and making amends for the hurt or loss that we have caused. These lessons are important because we are living in a generation where there is much personal irresponsibility.

"Irresponsibility" means to not be willing to be called into account for actions; to be unreliable. Someone is irresponsible when they fail to take responsibility for the actions they have committed.

Examples of irresponsibility are:

- Making excuses; you say, "No one's perfect."
- Rationalizing; you say, "Everybody is doing it."

Does the fact that "everybody else is doing it" make it right? Jesus said, "Wide and broad is the road that leads to destruction and there are many who go that way." Matthew 7:13

Do you remember when you were young and you wanted to do something but your parent did not agree? You would say, "But everyone else is doing it." And of course your mom would respond, "If they all walked off a cliff would you follow?"

There must be this University of Motherhood where they are taught, if your child says, "Everybody else is doing it," then you say, "If they all walked off a cliff would you do it too?" Because this seems to be the pat answer that mothers give to their children.

Rationalizing is failure to be responsible. Another example of irresponsibility is;

• Convenience – it was easier.

All of these things lead to sin. When we enter into sin, we always hurt somebody. No one ever sins to themself. If we make excuses, if we rationalize, if we take the convenient road, that doesn't justify what we've done. These courses of action never bring us to a higher level in life. They do not bring balance and practicality into our lives as God would have us to be.

Now, let's talk about taking responsibility with regard to those you've hurt. So far we have seen that God wants His people to be responsible for their actions. Now we will see how to do it.

Psalm 37:21 *The wicked borrows and does not pay back, but the righteous is gracious and gives.*

The "wicked" are immoral, irresponsible people. Here, the wicked borrows but are not responsible or accountable. They don't pay back what they've borrowed.

The act of "borrowing" signifies a debt/obligation. If you borrow money from someone, you have a debt, you are obligated to pay it back. If you borrow a tool from someone, you are obligated to give it back. If you break it you should replace it. That is balance and practicality. This is making amends for the things that we've done.

The Christian life is a very accountable life. You are more accountable as a Christian than you were before you became a Christian.

Therefore, whatever we borrow, whatever we use, whatever we break, whatever we hurt, that becomes something for which amends must be made.

When you hurt someone with words or deeds, you have incurred a debt. In order to go forward, you need to make amends with those you've hurt.

The early church in Jerusalem had some issues going on there and some of the people were divided against one another. The leader of the church, James told the people to *confess your sins <u>to one another</u>, and pray for one another...* James 5:16. This doesn't mean to tell the whole congregation what you've done wrong but it does mean to go to the person that you hurt and reconcile. Or go to the person that hurt you and reconcile. But don't let division stand in the church or in the family or in any other type of relationship.

Satan is the god of division. God is the God of unity. Jesus once prayed a prayer that we would be one as He and the Father were one. John 17:11 So when we do hurt each other we must make amends. This is a step toward deliverance, toward wholeness, healing and being complete.

"To cure the ills of life, we must be right with God and right with men." (William Barclay)

The Apostle John said we cannot love God who we cannot see if we cannot love our brother who we can see. I John 4:20 This is how God keeps us real.

An evidence of true repentance and conversion is found in;

> Acts 19:18 *And a number of those who had faith came and made a public statement of their sins and all their acts.*

Many of the people that were becoming saved were previously into sorcery, magic and witchcraft. When they became truly converted, they brought all of their stuff and made a public display of their confession by burning them.

When a person is truly converted to Christ, they start to do things differently. You begin to show that the things of the world have nothing in you any more. It's like you can't wait to get rid of them.

Pride begins to diminish and when humility reigns, we don't mind taking the blame, even if it is not our fault. When we are in the flesh we wait for people to come to us. When we are in the spirit we go to people. We seek after them because, *God so loved the world that He gave...* John 3:16. God sought after us. He had nothing to be guilty of. God needed no forgiveness.

Jesus said about Himself, *the Son of Man has come to seek and save that which is lost.* Luke 19:10 He came to make amends with us and yet, He did nothing wrong. When you are filled with His Spirit, you should have no problem confessing your faults, admitting your wrongs, reconciling and doing whatever it takes to reinstate oneness in that relationship.

Let's look at a man who actually made amends with those he hurt. Zaccheus is the poster boy for making amends with those you've hurt.

In Luke 19, Jesus is walking through Jericho and this guy named Zaccheus who had heard about Jesus was interested in seeing him. He climbed a tree where Jesus would be walking by because he was "small in stature." Luke 19:3

Jesus saw him in the tree and said;

v.5 *Zaccheus, hurry and come down, for today I must stay at your house.*

Jesus knew his name. Jesus seems to know a lot about Zaccheus. He knew that he was hiding up in the tree. This tells us, if you look for God, He will surely look for you. God is not hiding from anybody.

If you look for God, you will find Him

Well, Zaccheus hurried down and of course, people grumbled because Jesus was gracious and was going to dine with a sinner. Zaccheus was a tax collector employed by the Roman government, therefore, he was hated by his people.

Zaccheus was so touched by the Lord that he made this startling statement.

v.8 *Zaccheus stopped and said to the Lord, "Behold, Lord, half of my possessions I will give to the poor, and if I have defrauded anyone of anything, I will give back four times as much."*

Zaccheus was truly touched by Jesus. When you are touched by Jesus, you will do some radical things. You are not the same person anymore. It is impossible to be the same person after you have been touched by Christ. The person you were before you were touched by Christ has been changed. Zaccheus had truly changed. He is making amends with those he hurt.

Notice his two-fold speech:

- Half my possessions I will give to the poor.
- I will give back 4 times as much to those I have defrauded.

By nature we are all selfish. After a true conversion, life becomes more about others. He wants to help the unfortunate and wants to restore his reputation. When you are on the road to recovery, your reputation means a lot to you. Your compulsive behavior has destroyed your reputation. You can't be trusted anymore. You are full of lies and deceit. So you really have to do some things to regain your reputation.

What is the significance of Zaccheus returning four times back what he has taken?

In the book of Numbers 5:6-7 we have the answer to that question. It tells us if a man or woman defrauds or wrongs someone, they are to make full restitution and add one fifth for the damages. In other words, if someone defrauded someone else, he had to pay back one hundred percent of the damages plus one fifth or twenty percent.

Zaccheus was returning 400% (4 times as much). He went beyond what was required by the law. He has certainly made amends with those he hurt.

Can you put a price tag on your reputation or your character? Probably not. We need to go to any length to restore a good name.

The result was;

v.9 *And Jesus said to him, Today salvation has come to this house, because he, too, is a son of Abraham.*

Salvation means deliverance. Zaccheus was delivered from himself and his old ways of doing things. That's the biggest deliverance that one can find. We need to be delivered from ourselves. Our biggest dysfunctions come from the fact of who we are and our thinking with a carnal, sin nature.

It is always freeing to do the right thing.

Illustration:

In a church service in England years ago, several women were giving their testimonies. Another woman just sat grimly still. When asked to give her testimony, she refused.

When asked why, she answered, "Four of these women who have just given their testimony borrowed money from me and never repaid me, and I and my family are half-starved because we cannot buy food."

Principle:

A testimony is worthless unless it is backed up by deeds which guarantee its sincerity. Actions do speak louder than words. It is a lot of work to be restored back after the hurt caused by compulsive behaviors. That is why making amends is so important. At that stage of the game, words don't mean much anymore. People have heard it all. If you say you're a different person, let them see it in your life.

It is not mere words which Jesus demands but a change of life - "Balance & Practicality."

When one makes amends with those they've hurt, they are on their way to deliverance. Start to think, "Who am I on the outs with? Who have I hurt?" It may have been intentionally or unintentionally. You need to step out by faith and at least do your part. Even if you are not received, you have done your part and you are free. And if they do receive it, you have reconciled a relationship.

Make the commitment right now to make amends with the people that you've hurt.

Things I need to do

STEP 9

Having A
Servant's Heart

STEP 9
Having A Servant's Heart
Coming Out Of Your Own Life

"Having A Servant's Heart, Coming Out Of Your Own Life," is a principle of life contrary to what we do that gets us into trouble in the first place.

What gets people into trouble is "selfishness." Selfishness makes life all about me. Having the heart of a servant is contrary to being selfish. When I'm self-ish, it's all about the self. It becomes about how I feel, what I want, what I'm going through. This always gets us into trouble.

A servant's heart makes life all about someone else.

In this chapter, we will see what it is to be like Christ.

If you think about it, when Jesus went to the cross, His mind wasn't on Himself, it was on us. *For the joy that was set before Him, He endured the cross...*Hebrews 12:2 We were that joy. He was able to stay in a bad situation because He wasn't thinking about

Himself. He was thinking about others. That is the way out of the worst situation. Think about others and not yourself.

I Peter 2:18 *Servants, be submissive to your masters with all respect, not only to those who are good and gentle, but also to those who are unreasonable.*

When Peter addresses these people called servants, the word *(oiketes)* means a domestic or household slave. He is not using the word *(doulos)* which means a bondservant. A bondservant is one who serves because they owe a debt. They cannot pay the debt so they are put into slavery to work off the debt. Household servants were the servants that made up the greater part of the early church.

Christianity came into a world, the Roman world, where slaves were common property to the Romans. They were not treated harshly, many of them fulfilling roles as teachers, doctors, actors, musicians, secretaries and various workers. But they were treated like property because they were not citizens and numbered in the millions.

When James addressed his congregation in Jerusalem, he told the people not to make a distinction between the rich and the poor. In the early church, there were no class distinctions. Slaves and masters all attended church, many attended the same church. Into this world came the Gospel of Christ.

In the church, social barriers were broken down. It was even possible for a slave to be the leader of a congregation and his master a member in it.

It is in this backdrop that Peter urges the slave to be a good slave and faithful worker, because of;

Two dangers:

1. Both slave and master become Christians and the slave begins to shirk his duties. Even today there arises the problem sometimes of a Christian working for another Christian and the Christian employee doesn't take his job seriously. Both being Christians, he sometimes thinks he doesn't have to work that hard and would rather talk and fellowship. You are not getting paid to fellowship, you are getting paid to work.

A reminder to every employed Christian is that as a Christian, you should be the best worker on the job.

Peter is reminding the slaves not to shirk their responsibilities and to serve with the right heart, a servant's heart.

2. The second danger was that the slaves would rebel and seek to abolish slavery altogether. God is not the God of rebellions. God does teach us to "be content in whatever state we are in." Philippians 4:11. To encourage slaves to rise against their masters would mean certain disasters.

Peter is saying to the slaves, yes, you are born again and you are slaves. So fulfill the roles that have been given to you and maintain a servant's heart at all times. Don't let being a Christian stop you from being a servant. Christians should make the best servants because servant hood is so much like Christ. Our goal is to become as much like Christ as we possibly can.

By the way, Christian masters or bosses should also be the best masters and bosses at their roles.

Christian responsibility:

A Christian slave (someone with the heart of a servant) can certainly fulfill;

Colossians 3:23 *Whatever you do, do your work heartily, as for the Lord rather than for men,*

Realize that whatever you do, you are really doing it for God.

Christian duty:

The Christian has a duty to be a Christian within that situation and accept what cannot be changed. There are some things in our lives that will not change. So what do we do? We maintain the heart of a servant in that thing.

What introduced the compulsive behavior in the beginning was just the opposite. That was making life all about "me." And we make life all about "me" and things don't go our way, we start doing things to dull the pain, to get more control but we only end up with compulsive behaviors.

But if I can maintain the heart of a servant and make life about others, I'm not going to find myself wanting because life is not about "me." I can also find myself serving God by serving other people.

What happens when one who serves, lives life this way?

v.19 *For this finds favor, if for the sake of conscience toward God a person bears up under sorrows when suffering unjustly.*

If you feel like you are being treated unjustly, maintain the heart of a servant. Take it! That is something we do not like to do. We don't like to "take it."

We would rather fight it or change it. Fighting things or changing things never changes us. What changes us is bearing up under the pressure. When we bear up under the pressure, we get stronger.

A weight lifter bears up under the pressure and gets stronger. He adds more weight and bears up under more pressure and gets even stronger still. This is how you put on a servant's heart, by coming out of your own life because at the center of your life is the sin nature. You have to come out of that nature. The sin nature makes life all about me. When I come out of that into the divine nature, I am able to make life about others.

Jesus gave nobility to the role of servant hood. Until Christ came, servants were looked down upon. But when Christ came on the scene, He made serving noble. He is God and whatever God does is noble. He said, *I am not one who came to be served, but one who came to serve.* Mark 10:45

It takes self-confidence, great faith and knowing who you are in Christ to be a servant. Insecure people cannot serve because they're afraid their image might become tainted. People may look down upon them. They merely lack the confidence that serving requires. But when you have confidence in God and who God made you to be, there is nothing you won't do. That is real freedom.

Now, Christianity did not leave the matter in a merely negative form. It introduced three great principles of attitude and work.

> 1. Christianity introduced a new attitude between master and slave.

Master and slave are brothers in Christ. The Holy Spirit has bonded them and it doesn't matter which one is master or slave. Yes, on the job the master is the authority and the slave is the worker. The master should treat the slave with dignity because he is a brother in Christ. The slave should serve the master with all of his heart because he is a brother in Christ.

> 2. Christianity introduced a new attitude toward work.

As we just saw, everything must be done for Christ, not men.

Colossians 3:24 *knowing that from the Lord you will receive the reward of the inheritance. It is the Lord Christ whom you serve.*

Remember this when you are driving to work and thinking to yourself, "Oh, I hate my job, I hate my boss. I can't believe what I have to do today. Oh, I'm not looking forward to this." Remember that it is the Lord, Christ whom you serve. Whether driving a truck, digging a hole or making million dollar decisions, it is the Lord, Christ whom you serve. We are all serving God in the capacity that He has equipped us for our vocation. So we need to do the best that we can because we are doing it for Him.

In God's economy, work is not done:
- For an earthly master
- Personal prestige
- Just to make money

Rather, it is service to God and good for the soul.

When God created Adam He gave Him work to do, even though Adam was living in a perfect environment. The weather was perfect, the grass was green, it looked like it was treated with Scott's fertilizer, and Scott's fertilizer wasn't even invented yet. Everything was just beautiful. Yet, Adam was still given the job of working in the garden. But if everything was so perfect, why did Adam have to work? Because work is good for the soul. We have been created to be productive.

We have been created in the image of God and God works. He brought the whole creation into existence and He sustains it with the word of His power.

Hebrews 1:3

So when we do work, we must have the attitude that I am serving Him. And this attitude helps me to have a servant's heart. If you're at work and you wear a white shirt and tie and you go into the men's room and there are some papers on the floor, because you're serving God, you can pick them up.

If you were only working for the company you would just leave them for the janitor. But you're working for God. So you can pick up those little papers and make the place nice because a Christian always wants to leave where they were better after they've left than how it was before they got there.

There is no way in the world people will fall into compulsive behaviors when they're occupied with serving God and others and their mind is not on themselves all the time.

So, Christianity introduced a new attitude between:

1.   master and slave
2.   toward work
3.   It introduced a new attitude toward injustice and suffering.

v.20 *For what credit is there if, when you sin and are harshly treated, you endure it with patience?*

But if when you do what is right and suffer for it you patiently endure it, this finds favor with God.

You mean there are times in my life when I'm going to do the right thing and I'm going to suffer for doing it? The answer is, Yes. And when I suffer for doing the right thing and I patiently endure it, that finds favor with God? The answer is still, Yes.

Remember, a servant doesn't have any rights. The servant belongs to the master. The master makes all the decisions in the life of the servant.

There are things that are going to happen in our lives where we are going to say, "That's not fair, or that's not right, I don't deserve this. This shouldn't have happened." But God says if you can patiently endure, you will find favor with Me and I will give you grace.

In the next verse, Peter explains why.

v.21 *For you have been called for this purpose, since Christ also suffered for you, leaving you an example for you to follow in His steps.* We've been called to become like Christ. And a part of becoming like Christ is suffering by being treated unfairly.

When that happens, you have two choices.

1. You can stop the process of becoming like Christ by criticizing and complaining.

2. You can let the process continue and little by little become shaped and molded into the image of Christ. You are bearing up under it, patiently enduring it. You are not making it about you.

Notice what Jesus did:

V.22 *Who committed no sin, nor was any deceit found in His mouth.* This is while He was suffering. He never said a bad word. When is the last time you said a bad word? What did it take for you to say a bad word? It wasn't a nail through your hand or a crown of thorns on your head. Perhaps it was just the leg of a coffee table or a spilled drink on your lap. But for Jesus, even the crucifixion did not compel Him to sin.

A compulsive behavior is to lash back at people who upset you. Lashing out is a behavior that leads down a path of destruction. When you are upset with someone, the fire is already burning. So when you lash out, it is like throwing gasoline on the fire.

Did you ever enter into a lively discussion (argument) with someone? You are ready to say something and the little voice inside says, "Don't say it." But then you say it anyway because you are so upset. That really fixed it, didn't it? No, you just poured gas on a fire. That's what gets things flying across the room.

The Value of Dialogue

There are two challenges in problem solving today:

1. People do not know how to dialogue about a problem. Then it becomes a match of wits and decibels. Whoever can be the loudest, wins. Dialogue is civilly discussing with the intention of understanding the other person. That is the best way to solve problems, and yet, many people can't do that.

Instead, we have to be louder. We have to be right. We have to win. We have to put the other person in their place. Rather, if both parties don't win no one wins. If you have a winner and a loser in an argument, you have two losers. Nobody really wins. We have to be the kind of people that learn how to dialogue.

2. People withdraw from the problem. This is a calmer approach but it still doesn't solve the problem.

An unresolved issue is like a stone in your shoe. It hinders your walk. If a married couple has an unresolved issue they have a stone in their shoe and it hinders their walk together. If other issues are added that remain unresolved, the stones have built up. One day someone says, "I can't walk with you anymore. We've drawn apart."

Yet, if each issue could be resolved with proper dialogue, the problems would not escalate. All of this comes back to having the heart of a servant.

The servant doesn't have to win. The servant doesn't have to be right. The servant puts the other person first. This is why we need to look at Jesus.

V.23 *and while being reviled, He did not revile in return;*

"While being accused, He did not return the accusation." Sound familiar? One person makes an accusation about someone else and they fire right back, "Oh yeah, and what about you?"

Directly, they blame the other person. "It's your fault this happened. It's your fault I'm the way that I am."

Indirectly, they bring in a third party. They engage in the Adam and Eve syndrome of blaming others. Adam blamed Eve and Eve blamed the serpent. We can find ourselves blaming each other or blaming a third party, failing to take responsibility for our own lives. The servant always takes responsibility for their own life. When I take responsibility for my own life, I don't have to go down that road that leads to compulsive behaviors. I take responsibility for that thing and it's done. It's over. But a compulsive behavior is like a vacuum. It sucks you in and once you're in it's difficult to get out.

Think of these accusations being made against you and what would you do?

Jesus was accused of:

- Working for the devil Matthew 12:24
- Being a drunk and befriending sinners
Matthew 11:19
- Being out of His mind Mark 3:21
- Being illegitimate John 8:19

The result was;

while suffering, He uttered no threats,

In other words, "while suffering, He did not threaten."

And while hanging on the cross He said, "Father, forgive them..." He excused them for everything they said and everything they did.

v.23 *while suffering, He uttered no threats,* - this is the "difference maker". This is how you go from being in a place of suffering and not return the accusation, throw back the stone or defend yourself.

He kept entrusting Himself to Him who judges righteously;

Jesus kept Himself in the care of God.

The whole world was caving in on Jesus and He kept Himself in the care of God. He didn't seek to alleviate His pain by drinking, gambling, shopping or doing drugs. He didn't get on the phone and call ten friends to tell them how bad life is. No, He trusted Himself to the care of God, Who judges righteously.

Isaiah 26:3 *The LORD gives perfect peace to those whose faith is firm.* Contemporary English Version

Ask yourself, "Do I really have a firm faith?" Isn't that worth attaining when the whole world comes crashing down on you? Wouldn't it be great to have perfect peace? This is a peace that passes understanding. It is a peace that we can't even comprehend or explain. But somehow, someway, it finds its way into our heart and it stabilizes us. We can have perfect peace in the midst of a storm. God gives that to people who continue to trust Him.

If I have a firm faith , then I can do these things.

1. I can have a servant's heart.

This will allow me to come out of myself and to really begin to live for God.

2. I will have a new attitude toward work.

From now on, it is the Lord, Jesus I serve.

3. I will see suffering and injustice in a new way.

It happened to Christ and it must happen to me if I am going to be like Him.

Then;

4. I can put my life in God's hands.

If I continually trust Him, He will continue to keep me peaceful because my mind is not on myself or others but it is on Him.

This is how to have a servant's heart and come out of your own life

Things I need to do

STEP 10

Taking A
Continual
Inventory

STEP 10:
Taking A Continual Inventory
Persevering

When you think of recovering lost ground, you must remember it is a life long process. The Christian life of becoming like Christ is also a life long process.

Mastering an instrument or any art form is a life long process. I guess you could say, anything worth becoming your best at is going to require a life long journey.

Like any journey, every once in a while, you have to stop and check your bearings.

On the highway, we have rest areas. In rest areas, you can find these huge bulletin boards with a glass front. Under the glass are large maps of the area you are traveling through. Somewhere in the middle is a little red star that says, "You are here." From there, you can determine the course your journey must take.

At sea, you follow your charts. Your charts will tell you where you are, how to get to where you are going and the hazards along the way. And so it is with growing in Christ.

While growing in Christ we take an inventory, not once in a while but consistently.

II Corinthians 13:5 *Test yourselves to see if you are in the faith; examine yourselves! Or do you not recognize this about yourselves, that Jesus Christ is in you...*

This is a continual inventory that we have to take. This is what Step 10 is about.

STEP 10
Taking A Continual Inventory

When taking an inventory of myself, I am asking myself, "Where am I, how am I doing, am I getting closer to my destination?"

Now, during this life long process, there will be times of pain, disappointment and various emotions.

I remember taking a 118' mission ship to Haiti, it took about 3 days to get there.

There were times of relaxation because it was beautiful cruising. Sometimes it was scary because the waves were breaking over the pilot house. Other times, it was boredom, especially if we had to stop somewhere and make repairs.

All kinds of emotions accompanied the journey to our destination. And you have to realize that in your life long journey, you are going to experience all kinds of emotions. Yes, there will be disappointment. There will be joy. There will be pain and a whole range of other emotions, so what you have to do is stay with it. No one reaches their destination when they quit before they get there. That's the problem with so many people today. Too many people quit before they get to where they want to be.

In II Timothy 2, Paul describes to young Timothy what he can expect in his journey in ministry. He gives him five things to do to help him keep a check on himself, or take a continual inventory on how he is doing.

v.1 Be strong.

Be strong in the grace that is in Jesus Christ

Paul is telling Timothy to always be strong in grace because that is where God puts His strength into you. He provides the strength you need, so live in it!

I can do all things through Him who strengthens me. Philippians 4:13

2. Suffer Hardship.

v.3 <u>*Suffer hardship with me*</u>*, as a good soldier of Christ Jesus.*

Sometimes we think our Christian journey is not supposed to be difficult.

Paul said "suffer hardship <u>'with me</u>.'" He is saying, "I'm suffering hardship too." Hardship is the norm in the Christian life. We have to expect it. To "suffer hardship in company with," means they are both experiencing the same thing, hardship.

The great apostle suffered hardship, so why wouldn't we.

Suffer hardship with me as a good soldier... the word "good" *kalos* means an observable good. It is a good that you can see.

Matthew 5:16 *Let your light shine before men in such a way that they may <u>see your good works</u>, and glorify your Father who is in heaven.*

Suffer as a good soldier or a warrior. Note the word is not spelled "worrier" but "warrior." There is a difference. Paul often used this term to describe those in the Christian life who are fighting the good fight of faith.

II Corinthians 10:3 *We do not war according to the flesh* because behind personal conflict is demonic activity. Fiery darts come from the enemy into the mind and cause wrong thinking.

Philippians 2:25 *Epaphroditus, my brother, fellow worker and fellow soldier.*

Ephesians 6:11 *Put on the full armor of God.* Armor is for warfare.

Therefore, on your journey to overcome a compulsive behavior, you are going to encounter a battle. You have to ask yourself if you are in it for the long haul. Am I going to stay with it until I get to the end, or is something going to trip me up and I fall away from the battle? This is why we need to take a continual moral inventory and see if we are operating according to the faith. Am I on course? Am I going in the proper direction? Am I ready for any opposition that might face me? Warfare implies hardship.

3. Follow the rules.

v.5 *Also if anyone competes as an athlete, he does not win the prize unless he competes according to the rules.*

The ancient athletes lived for nothing else but the Olympic games. That was their goal in life. The Olympics were so important to the ancient cultures that they would cease from warring with each other when the time for the games rolled around. When the games were over, they went back to fighting.

The athletes had to train and know the rules of their sport.

So it is with the life of the Christian. He or she can let nothing get in the way of their training. If you are serious about becoming all that God would have you to be, then you have to live for that.

For the ancient athletes, their strength, agility, coming in first and even zealousness does not matter in comparison to "following the rules." If the athlete did not follow the rules of the game, he was disqualified.

- A foul ball homerun is not a home run.
- A touchdown from running through the stands is not a touchdown.

Think with me for a minute.

Many lives have become shipwrecked because they had to do it "their way." They forgot the rules. They made up their own rules. Doing it their way is what got them into trouble in the first place. Most of the trouble we make for ourselves is because we have to do it our way. And yet, many people are unwilling to do whatever it takes to be made well. They actually allowed pleasures and indulgences in their training.

I was working with a man recently who had a serious battle with alcohol. I got him into a program and he left. A few days later I got him back into the same program and he left again. He didn't want to go by their rules but he wanted his own rules. He forgot that it was his own standards and rules that got Him into trouble in the first place. You must submit yourself to God and in humility, do whatever it is you have to do.

Are you willing, right now, to admit that you will do whatever it takes so you can get the victory over your compulsive behavior?

If so, then sign your name right here and date it.

———————————————————————

How many compulsive behaviors are never defeated because people had to do it their way and not the hard way? They fail to realize that living in their compulsive behavior is really the hard way. Sleeping in the street, that's the hard way. Getting the DTs, that's the hard way. Living in dirty clothes, that's the hard way. Being estranged from family and friends, that's the hard way.

I guess at this stage, if you're not willing to do whatever it takes, you will go no farther. This is the end of the road.

4. Expect a reward.

v.6 *The hard-working farmer ought to be the first to receive his share of the crops.*

Paul is not talking about any farmer but the "hard working" farmer. There is a reward to the individual who is "hard-working" at their recovery. Nothing is easy that is worth going after.

A farmer must be good at two things:

1. working

2. waiting

He works hard preparing the ground, sowing the seed and cultivating the crop. Then, he waits for the increase.

Yet, *Those who wait upon the Lord will renew their strength...* Isaiah 40:31

Also, farming is not a convenient vocation. It involves early risings, long hours and difficult tasks. But the result is an abundant harvest.

There is one thing the soldier, athlete and hard working farmer all have in common. The solider is upheld by the thought of final victory. The athlete is inspired by the vision of the crown. The hard-working farmer is encouraged by the hope of the harvest.

What they have in common is, each one submits to the discipline and toil required for the sake of the glory that will be.

For you, the struggle is not without a goal. The goal is the joy of deliverance from this behavior and ultimately from this earth.

So far Paul said to Timothy;

      1. Be strong in grace
      2. Suffer hardship
      3. Follow the rules
      4. Expect a reward

Finally,

5. Remember these things.

v.7 *Consider what I say, for the Lord will give you understanding in everything.*

The word "consider" *noieo* means to exercise the mind, to comprehend. This is important because we often hear something that will benefit us but it only takes moments before it is forgotten.

Note Jesus' parable of the sower in Luke 8:5-18.

(You can find this account in the back of this book.)

Paul is saying to Timothy, exercise your mind regarding these illustrations I just gave you. The images of the soldier, athlete and hard working farmer will stay with you because they are in your everyday life.

1. Think about God's grace strengthening you.
2. Expect some hardship to come.
3. Stay in the rules and don't try to do everything your way. God has a game plan.
4. Work hard at it and you will be rewarded just like the soldier, athlete and farmer.
5. Consider what you just learned.

Don't leave this chapter and pick up the junk you left when you began to read. Don't be consumed with your junk instead of the things that you just learned. Be consumed with the things that God is saying.

This is the continual inventory we must take of ourselves. This is the course we take, the charts we follow. Remember and do these things and expect a favorable outcome.

Things I need to do

STEP 11

Finding God And
Sticking With Him

STEP 11
Finding God & Sticking With Him
Remembering

As we arrive at Step 11, we come to a place of great importance, yet, it is something that many people fail to do. Sometimes the most important things are the things that we fail to do.

I think of 3 categories of people:

1. Those who don't find God at all. Believe it or not, there are people who just haven't found God and don't know if they ever will.

2. Those who do find Him but don't stick with Him.

3. Those who find Him and do stick with Him.

Let's seek to be in this third category. Ask yourself, "Do I want to be in the category of those who find God, but not only find God but stick with Him?"

As we've been going through this recovery process, we spent a lot of time looking back over your life at the things you've done.

We talked about how:

- How arrogant thinking got us into trouble.
- The need to make better choices.
- Godly sorrow that leads to repentance.
- Receiving forgiveness for what we've done.
- Being honest before God.
- Making amends with those we've hurt.
- Taking on a servant's heart.

Now, we are going to take the focus off of ourselves and put it on God.

Psalm 105:1-4 The Psalmist shows us how he finds God.

v.1 *Oh <u>give thanks</u> to the LORD, <u>call upon His name</u>; <u>Make known His deeds</u> among the people.*

v.2 *<u>Sing to Him</u>, sing praises to Him; Speak of all His wonders.*

v.3 *<u>Glory in His holy name</u>; Let the heart of those who seek the LORD be glad.*

v.4 *<u>Seek the LORD and His strength</u>; <u>Seek His face</u> continually.*

We have so many things here:

- Be thankful to the Lord. You can be thankful to the Lord when you take the focus off of yourself and put it on Him. You cannot "but" be thankful when you put your mind on God.
- Pray. When you talk to God in prayer, the focus is coming off you and it is going on Him.
- Sing "to" Him. Worship is singing to God. That should fill your singing with passion.

Did you ever pull up to a red light and see the driver sitting next to you and they are just belting out a song? Perhaps it was their favorite song. Oh, they were just singing away, hands moving, head bobbing.

Singing excites an emotion and when you're singing to God, you are singing to the greatest audience.

•Glory. Boast about the name of God. Praise His "name."

Acts 4:12 *There is salvation in no one else; for there is no other name under heaven that has been given among men by which we must be saved.*

There is no name like "Jesus Christ." Don't become familiar with it or bring shame to it.

•Seek. This is an important part of recovery. Even when you feel at your worst, seek after God.

Oftentimes, when we feel at our worst, we want to hurt ourselves. But that's the time you want to seek after God. When people feel at their worst, they don't care about themselves. They do things that hurt themselves, and they don't care. When you seek after God, you're seeking after Someone who cares about you, though at that moment, you may not care about yourself.

The psalmist is looking back at the mighty deeds of God. This is a beautiful way to get one's mind off of self.

v.5 *Remember His wonders which He has done, His marvels and the judgments uttered by His mouth,*

His "wonders and marvels" are the same Hebrew word which speak of miracles, signs and wonders. The psalmist is getting the readers of his day to remember what God had done previously in their history.

Ex.

•Parting the Red Sea, remember that deliverance. It was an impossible situation for the people of Israel, but not for God. Exodus 14:16

• Stopping the Jordan River, remember their advance. At that time the river was running at its highest, deepest and fastest. Joshua 4

• Causing the sun to stand still, remember that battle. The day was lengthened to give God's people the victory. Joshua 10:12

The psalmist wants us to know that God may ask you to do the impossible but He will see you through.

On this note, we need to realize that God will come through for us too.

Can you think of some times where God has spared you or come through for you in the past? Name them.

Perhaps it was an accident that didn't happen. Maybe it was a sickness that didn't worsen. It could have been an argument that never took place.

Now, let's bring it back to our 3 categories of people:

1. Those who don't find Him.

2. Those who do find Him but don't stick with Him.

3. Those who find Him and stick with Him.

I hope category no.1 is not true for you. If you are in category no.1 you can ask God right now to reveal Himself to you. He always honors a sincere heart of humility.

You can read John 3:16 *For God so loved the world that He sent His only begotten Son that whoever believes in Him would never perish, but have everlasting life.* This can be the beginning of your new life in God.

Observation has shown that category no.2 is the one found with many people, even Christians. They seek Him, find Him, but they don't stick with Him.

How easy we forget God:

- in times of trial some people will fall away.
- in times of recovery some people will not want to do the hard work.
- in times of prosperity some people forget their need for God.

Examples:

In times of trial we become like the disciples in the boat in the storm. At that moment they stopped walking in their faith. They cried out, *Master, we perish!* Matthew 8:24-25

In times of recovery we may become like Elijah and run for fear of what may happen. Elijah ran for his life because he received a threatening letter and he feared the future. This happened after a tremendous victory brought by God on his behalf. I Kings 19:2-3

In recovery, people do not continue with the process because they fear what would be exposed or what they may be required to do. Maybe it's what they would have to do. Fear will never help your progress, in anything! Fear is one of the top three stumbling stones to the Christian, doubt and sin being the other two.

In times of prosperity we become like the man who built bigger barns. Luke 12:18

It doesn't make sense to walk away from God after He blesses you but people do it all the time. Prosperity is abundance for the purpose of helping others. We have to be careful that prosperity doesn't take away our need for God. God wants to be first and foremost in our lives whether in need or abundance.

The question in recovery is not "Have I found God?" but "Have I found God and am I sticking with Him?"

Third category:

3. Those who find Him and stick with Him.

Psalm 1:1 This person takes Godly advice. If you are carnal or natural minded, Godly advice is going to offend you.

How blessed is the man who does not walk in the counsel of the wicked, Nor stand in the path of sinners, Nor sit in the seat of scoffers!

Anything wicked is contrary to God's wisdom.

v.2 He finds pleasure in God's Word and thinks about it often

But his delight is in the law of the LORD, And in His law he meditates day and night.

This person is thankful for what the Word of God is telling him.

v.3 He is stable in storms. Therefore, he lives a fruitful life and is prosperous.

He will be like a tree firmly planted by streams of water, which yields its fruit in its season and its leaf does not wither; and in whatever he does, he prospers.

Be a Psalm 1 individual.

Take advice from Godly people. Find pleasure in the Word of God. And God will make you stable in the storm.

So with all that you may have gone through, this is a good time to start looking forward by looking at God. It's time to get eyes off self, eyes off the past. At this stage, we begin to get our eyes on God and stick with Him.

Things I need to do

STEP 12

Sharing Your
Story With Others

STEP 12
Sharing Your Story With Others
Telling Others What God Has Done

Much of what we learned in the first 11 steps of Recovering Lost Ground was with the intention of deriving personal benefit.

But this final step, Step 12, is more for the benefit of others. This is where we proclaim what God has done and how He turns a curse into a blessing.

People find themselves in difficult places. But when they give their life to God and He gets a hold of them, He takes their curse and turns it into a beautiful blessing. Then, it becomes a blessing to others when they share the story of what God has done for them.

The sharing of the story of the work of God was also the last command that Jesus gave to His disciples before He ascended into heaven.

Picture the life of Christ on earth:

•Three years of ministry together with the disciples.

- The performing of signs and wonders together.
  - Healing the sick and feeding the hungry.
  - Forgiving the guilty.
  - Comforting the afflicted.
  - Telling the good news of the Kingdom.

Jesus has finished the work He had been given to do. He died on a cross and was buried in a tomb. Three days later He rose from the grave, gathered His disciples together and gave them this command.

It's been said the last thing a person says before they leave is the most important thing.

Picture yourself on your own deathbed. Your loved ones are all around you. And you have the blessing of telling them what you consider to be the most important thing in life. What would you tell them?

Jesus gathers His disciples and gives them this final command.

Mark 16:15 *Go into all the world and preach the gospel to all creation.* For that to be the last thing that Jesus said means that must be the dearest thing to Jesus' heart.

The "gospel" is the story of the work that Christ accomplished in paying the debt for the sins of the world.

He defeated Satan, God's adversary, and now offers forgiveness and eternal life to all who believe in Him.

v.16 *He who has believed and has been baptized shall be saved; but he who has disbelieved shall be condemned.* This is the message that Jesus wants communicated to all creation.

Faith is the means to attaining salvation not baptism. Baptism, as commanded by God, is the evidence that one has believed. It is evidence because it is obedience to the command of God. If we are not obedient to the commands of God, how can we say that we have truly believed?

Matthew 7:21 *Not everyone who says to Me, 'Lord, Lord,' will enter the kingdom of heaven, but he who does the will of My Father who is in heaven will enter.*

Faith is the basis of salvation and obedience is the evidence of that salvation.

v.16 *but he who has disbelieved shall be condemned.*

The importance of telling your story.

Your story is a story of deliverance from bondage and sin. It is a story of freedom and redemption. It's that which gives hope for the future and confidence in the present.

The Gospel is the story of Christ; who He is and what He did in the world. But your story is who God is "in your life," and how He set you free. Perhaps He has set you free was from a bad practice of a habitual sin. He may have given you your freedom from that compulsive behavior. Or He set you free from poor self-worth or low self-esteem. He delivered you and filled you with life. He put your feet upon a Rock and gave you stability.

Let's take a look at this principle in action.

In Acts 26, The Apostle Paul travelled the world telling his conversion story. A big part of the Apostle Paul's ministry was telling people what God had done in his life. But wouldn't you know it. At the end of his life, he finds himself in chains before King Agrippa. He was

Jewish but made king by the Romans. As Paul stands before King Agrippa, he shares his story.

Background:
- He grew up Jewish
- Became a Pharisee of the strictest sect
- Was hostile to the name of Jesus of Nazareth

v.10 He shares his story

And this is just what I did in Jerusalem; not only did I lock up many of the saints in prisons, having received authority from the chief priests, but also when they were being put to death I cast my vote against them.

v:11 And as I punished them often in all the synagogues, I tried to force them to blaspheme; and being furiously enraged at them, I kept pursuing them even to foreign cities. This is where Paul was before God changed him. He hated people just because of what they believed in their hearts. This is the basis of religious persecution.

v.12 While so engaged as I was journeying to Damascus with the authority and commission of the chief priests,

v.13 at midday, O King, I saw on the way a light from heaven, brighter than the sun, shining all around me and those who were journeying with me.

v.14 And when we had all fallen to the ground, I heard a voice saying to me in the Hebrew dialect, "Saul, Saul, why are you persecuting Me? It is hard for you to kick against the goads."

Rebelling against the plan of God is painful. Paul then wonders if this is God who he is persecuting. Paul is going to discover that he was wrong. What a terrible feeling it is to believe you have been right but then find out you've been wrong!

v.15 *And I said, 'Who are You, Lord?' And the Lord said, "I am Jesus whom you are persecuting."*

Paul then had a revelation of who Christ truly was. He began to relate the change that Christ brought into his life.

v.19 *So, King Agrippa, I did not prove disobedient to the heavenly vision,*

v.20 *but kept declaring both to those of Damascus first, and also at Jerusalem and then throughout all the region of Judea, and even to the Gentiles, that they should repent and turn to God, performing deeds appropriate to repentance.*

v.21 *For this reason some Jews seized me in the temple and tried to put me to death.*

Paul is now on the receiving end of persecution.

v.22 *So, <u>having obtained help from God</u>,* There it is. This is the key verse for the overcomer. The one that overcame compulsive behavior is the one who got help from God.

Now, this is your story.

"I was stuck in this addiction. I was stuck in this lifestyle, in this way of dulling the pain. But I received help from God. God did a work in me. He delivered me and strengthened me. God made me a brand new creation." That is your testimony to share with others.

Paul continued.

I stand to this day testifying both to small and great, stating nothing but what the Prophets and Moses said was going to take place;

Then, He relates the story of the Christ and His resurrection.

Even the great, Apostle Paul shared his story of what God had done in his life.

v.28 *Agrippa replied to Paul, "In a short time you will persuade me to become a Christian."*

People can deny and argue about the Bible but there is no denying a changed life.

v.29 *And Paul said, "I would wish to God, that whether in a short or long time, not only you, but also all who hear me this day, might become such as I am, except for these chains."*

Paul desired that all who heard his story would become like him; a follower of Jesus Christ. He doesn't want them to share his chains but his freedom in Christ.

The story of the journey from bondage to freedom is the story of the Gospel. And each of us has the potential to experience that story.

When you share your story, you are offering others the chance to shed their own chains and begin a life of recovery, freedom and redemption.

I believe that everyone that is not "born again" John 3:3 is in some type of bondage. They are certainly in bondage to the power of sin. When they let the power of sin control their lives, they become in bondage to guilt. Sometimes guilt and shame becomes overwhelming. They lead to bondage to something else that they think will dull the pain. They may fall into some kind of abuse; substance abuse, gambling, shopping, over-eating. There are countless compulsive behaviors that people fall into in order to dull the pain that comes from sin.

Your story will help people to become free from that. When God set you free, it shows them God can set them free as well.

The Bible tells us;

We have a chief priest who is able to sympathize with our weaknesses. He was tempted in every way that we are, but He didn't sin. Hebrews 4:15

Jesus felt what we felt and hurt like we hurt. He knew the human experience. He can identify with us in our own affliction. Jesus knew what it was to be misunderstood, lied about, ostracized, and called illegitimate. Many believe He lost His father while He was still young. So Jesus knows what it is to grow up with a single mother. He knows what it is to be the oldest brother in the family and be the sole supporter of the family. He knows what it is to have His family not understand Him in His relationship with God. He knows what it is to do good and then be condemned for it. Jesus understands the human experience because He's been there. So He knows what it is to be you.

The only difference, is, He never sinned. When He was tempted or hurting, He didn't go to the casino or to the local bar. He didn't go to the mall. He went to His heavenly Father. That is how He got the victory. Jesus is saying, "You can get the victory just like I did."

Jesus knew ahead of time what His mission consisted of:

The Spirit of the Lord GOD is upon me, because the LORD has anointed me to bring good news to the afflicted; He has sent me to bind up the brokenhearted, to proclaim liberty to captives And freedom to prisoners; Isaiah 61:1

When Jesus read those Scriptures, He was reading about Himself. He knew, "This is about Me. This is My mission. This is My purpose on this earth."

Paul is telling the story of Jesus and he is telling his own story as well.

Jesus is not arrogant toward us but compassionate. Know that whatever you are struggling with, God is a compassionate God. He understands your struggle. He knows it's hard for you. He knows you're fighting a battle. He is for you and the Bible tells us that He prays for us. He wants you to be an over-comer.

When Christ shared His story, many people found hope. His story was a little different from ours. His story was the message of His death, burial and resurrection. That was His story. But, Jesus was delivered from the grave!

It was the personal stories of these great men that changed the world. How much do you believe your personal story can change the life of one person? It doesn't take a lot. You don't have to be a theologian. All you have to know is what God did for you.

You know your story and your testimony. "He picked me up out of the muck and the mire. I was in the worst place. And God picked me up and he cleaned me off and He put me on a Rock. He put His life into me and He restored me. He gave me grace and forgiveness. He gave me a brand new identity, in Him. He washed away all my sins, all my failures; they're gone and I never have to answer to God again for anything I've done wrong or will do in the future. That's what God has done for me. And God can do this for you. And not only can God do this for you, He wants to. He wants to do this for you because He wants you in heaven with Him.

And He wants you to live a full life on this earth. It might not be a long life, but it can be a full life. A full life has significance, purpose and value. A full life is not caught up in the stream where most people are floating downstream to their destruction."

So you just let them know what God has done for you and let the Holy Spirit go to work.

The Holy Spirit brings it to their heart and their understanding. And when they respond, God puts it in them to go to someone else and share their story. This is how it works.

Now it's time for you to share your story. In doing so, many others will find hope for their own lives and possibly even recover some lost ground.

Things I need to do

BIBLE PROMISES

Good Company

Iron sharpens iron, So one man sharpens another. Pr 27:17

He who walks with wise men will be wise, But the companion of fools will suffer harm. Pr 13:20

Meditation

The law of his God is in his heart; His steps do not slip. Ps 37:31

Overcomers

To him who overcomes, I will grant to eat of the tree of life which is in the Paradise of God. Rev 2:7

Patience

So that you will not be sluggish, but imitators of those who through faith and patience inherit the promises. Heb 6:12

Perseverance

Let us not lose heart in doing good, for in due time we will reap if we do not grow weary. Gal 6:9

Speech

He who guards his mouth and his tongue, Guards his soul from troubles. Pr 21:23

A soothing tongue is a tree of life, But perversion in it crushes the spirit. Pr 15:4

Success

How blessed is the man who does not walk in the counsel of the wicked, Nor stand in the path of sinners, Nor sit in the seat of scoffers! Ps 1:1

He will be like a tree *firmly* planted by streams of water, Which yields its fruit in its season And its leaf does not wither; And in whatever he does, he prospers. Ps 1:3

Trials

Consider it all joy, my brethren, when you encounter various trials, knowing that the testing of your faith produces endurance. And let endurance have *its* perfect result, so that you may be perfect and complete, lacking in nothing. Ja 1:2-4

Watchfulness

How blessed is the man who fears always, But he who hardens his heart will fall into calamity. Pr 28:14

Therefore let him who thinks he stands take heed that he does not fall. I Cor 10:12

David P. Therrien

Parable of the Sower
Luke 8:8-15

Lu 8:5 The sower went out to sow his seed; and as he sowed, some fell beside the road, and it was trampled under foot and the birds of the air ate it up.

v.6 Other seed fell on rocky soil, and as soon as it grew up, it withered away, because it had no moisture.

v.7 "Other seed fell among the thorns; and the thorns grew up with it and choked it out.

v.8 Other seed fell into the good soil, and grew up, and produced a crop a hundred times as great." As He said these things, He would call out, "He who has ears to hear, let him hear."

v.9 His disciples began questioning Him as to what this parable meant.

v.10 And He said, "To you it has been granted to know the mysteries of the kingdom of God, but to the rest it is in parables, so that seeing they may not see, and hearing they may not understand.

v.11 "Now the parable is this: the seed is the word of God.

v.12 "Those beside the road are those who have heard; then the devil comes and takes away the word from their heart, so that they will not believe and be saved.

v.13 Those on the rocky soil are those who, when they hear, receive the word with joy; and these have no firm root; they believe for a while, and in time of temptation fall away.

v.14 "The seed which fell among the thorns, these are the ones who have heard, and as they go on their way they are choked with worries and riches and pleasures of this life, and bring no fruit to maturity.

vb.15 "But the seed in the good soil, these are the ones who have heard the word in an honest and good heart, and hold it fast, and bear fruit with perseverance.

ABOUT THE AUTHOR

David P. Therrien

Graduated from Gordon Conwell Seminary in Boston, MA with a Masters of Arts Degree In Urban Ministry. He enjoys the four seasons of New England with his wife, Donna and has three sons, Michael, David Jr. and Alex.

Dave writes on matters of faith and encouragement and pastors the wonderful people of New Hope Christian Church in Swansea, MA.

www.newhopecc.tv

Other Resources
You can find other books by
David P. Therrien
at
www.inspiringbooks.org

Email
Inspiringbooksofhope@gmail.com

For CDs and DVDs go to
www.newhopecc.tv

POCKETBOOK SERIES
So far...

Look Up And Be Forgiven VOL.1
Going Forward In Faith VOL.2
How To Escape From Guilt & Shame VOL.3
Grace, Kindness & Righteousness VOL. 4
The Loving Father & The Lost Son VOL. 5
ALSO
Beauty In Darkness, Finding HOPE In Distressing Times
GOT Life?
Angel Conversations

169